FROM

Folly TO Faith

One Person's Journey from Pain to Promise

Denise DesGroseilliers Britton

From Folly to Faith: One Person's Journey from Pain to Promise

Trilogy Christian Publishers
A Wholly Owned Subsidiary of Trinity Broadcasting Network
2442 Michelle Drive, Tustin, CA 92780

For information, address Trilogy Christian Publishing Rights Department, 2442 Michelle Drive, Tustin, CA 92780. Trilogy Christian Publishing/ TBN and colophon are trademarks of Trinity Broadcasting Network. For information about special discounts for bulk purchases, please contact Trilogy Christian Publishing.

Trilogy Disclaimer: The views and content expressed in this book are those of the author and may not necessarily reflect the views and doctrine of Trilogy Christian Publishing or the Trinity Broadcasting Network.

10 9 8 7 6 5 4 3 2 1
Library of Congress Cataloging-in-Publication Data is available.
Manufactured in the United States of America

ISBN: 978-1-68556-490-2
e-ISBN: 979-8-88738-336-1

Dedication

To my husband, Jim,
son, Martin,
and daughters, Ashley and Janelle,
who stuck with me even though they experienced much
of the folly part of this journey!

Folly is an unruly woman;
She is simple and knows nothing.
                                    Proverbs 9:13-14 (NIV)

The fear of the Lord is the beginning of wisdom,
and knowledge of the Holy One is understanding.
                                    Proverbs 9:10-12

Forward

BY HAROLD HERRING

"The Christian experience, from start to finish, is a journey of faith."

— Watchman Nee

If I want to be honest, much of the success of my journey through life rests in the books I've read.

Some of the books were so profound that even now, years later, I can quote some of the thought-provoking, life-changing words I read.

Such is the case with *From Folly to Faith* written by an anointed, articulate wordsmith and faithful friend, Denise Britton. It's a book I will quote for years to come and so will you.

If you need hope, you picked up the right book because Denise delivers. She will give you hope where there has been none. Life-changing hope for your future.

Philemon 1:6 in God's WORD Translation says:

"As you share the faith you have in common with others, I pray that you may come to have a complete knowledge of every blessing we have in Christ."

Every blessing we have in Christ.

Feeling stuck? Need a way out of a seemingly impossible situation. This book shows you your way out.

Denise offers stellar advice about how to transform from what the world says is success to the lasting success God can bring to pass in your life.

Moving in faith enables and empowers each of us to experience every blessing we have in Christ.

1 Timothy 6:12 in the Classic Amplified Bible says:

> *"Fight the good fight of the faith. Take hold of the eternal life to which you were called when you made your good confession in the presence of many witnesses."*

In Denise's book you will be taught how to fight the good fight, to wage effective warfare, to tear down strongholds which is a result of FOLLOWING GOD'S INSTRUCTIONS.

You are called to fight the good fight of faith every day.

Hebrews 11:1 says:

> *"Now faith is the substance of things hoped for, the evidence of things not seen."*

What you "hoped for" is invisible, *but faith* is the evidence that makes it real.

You can't go into a courtroom and win a case with invisible evidence. When you take God's Word into the courtroom of Heaven you win every time.

If you want to be set free from abuse or other negatives that plagued you in the past, it may seem impossible… until you begin to see yourself free in the spirit.

In *From Folly To Faith* is: "A Penny For Your Thoughts." Consider the thought Denise shares:

> *"Penny for my thoughts? With each penny I would see and pick up, my thought was "In God I Trust"—and I learned to effectively give my thoughts to the Lord, for a penny!"*

A great way to start. And start you must if you want to be free!

> *"Yes indeed, it won't be long now." God's Decree. Things are going to happen so fast your head will swim, one thing fast on the heels of the other. You won't be able to keep up. Everything will be happening at once—and everywhere you look, blessings…"*
>
> Amos 9:13 (MSG)

Harold Herring

Acknowledgments

Diving into the journey, I would be remiss if I did not extend my personal thanks and appreciation to persons who have been so instrumental in helping me to take steps forward.

The early part of the journey, that I remember most vividly, began with the birth of my son, Martin Michael Lacki. Becoming a mom sparked something in me that became an ongoing inspiration to push through whatever might come, push past the depths of darkness I did not realize at the time was trying to cover me.

The births of my daughters, Ashley Suzanne and Janelle Louise, inspired me to consider what kind of life I would want to insure they could have, as girls and women—and how, if possible, I could help them to know *it is possible* to navigate life with confidence and empowerment, maintaining grace and compassion. They would not have to sell themselves out as women. Confidence and assertiveness do not equate to aggressiveness and boorishness, a lesson I had to learn having grown up in what could be described as a "stereotypic man's world" environment. With all due respect to men, I am grateful to the Holy Spirit for the testosterone interruption that led me back to a mindset where I could embrace being female, and still know that creating a positive future was very much in my grasp!

To my husband, Jim—as a CPA and driven by numbers and details, learning to accept the value in all of that helped me (sometimes kicking and screaming) I am forever grateful and value the love we have learned to share by a God we continue to get to know and hold in the center of our relationship.

To my mother who has supported me in ways I could never fully express, my Godfather, Uncle Roy DesGroseilliers (now with the Lord), my brothers Steve (now with the Lord), Stan and Rich; to Donna Shuler, Chris and Carol Green, Michele Smith, the team at Centurion Construction, the amazing women in the Harrisburg-Hershey Zonta Club, Lauren and Tom Zimmerman, Mona Stenz, our motley crew from the University of Dayton, and many others that were encouraging and faithful even amidst circumstances that were at times most trying, I extend my heartfelt gratitude. The journey with opportunities to gain and expand perspective included the welcoming of new persons into our family, Andrea Moore and Jonah Mooney, and beautiful grandchildren, Casey, Lydia and Brandon. Through the most challenging times of the journey, the establishment of the foundation of faith would become most clearly evidenced through relationships, existing and emerging, as truly unconditional love would become corner-stone of my life forever forward.

I need to acknowledge Neale Donald Walsch and his *Conversations with God* series of books that led me not only to consider the idea that God was approachable; it also led to an introduction to the author, actor and environmentalist, Dennis Weaver, founder of the Institute of Ecolonomics. One day, when I meet Dennis again in heaven, I will be able to share with him how much it meant to me to serve on the Board of Directors of the Institute of Ecolonomics (see https://ecolonomics.org) and to discover that it was possible to break through the worldly ideas that there is any separation among people (due to economic or other differences) that are not devised by man himself. I extend gratitude and appreciation to a full listing of ministries and mentors to include but not limited to the Debt Free Army, Kenneth Copeland Ministry, TBN, Paula White Ministry, Breakthrough, Creflo Dollar Ministry, Bill Winston Ministry, Keith Moore Ministry, Jerry Sevelle Ministries, Terry Sevelle Ministries, Eagle Mountain International Church, The Potters' House, and Joyce Meyer.

Introduction

This was the message in a church service in early September 2019. Messages from the spiritual families that have surrounded me for so many years were all centered on the message of "dunamis" power (Matthew 7:22, 11:21; Acts 8:13).

On first glance, it could seem like these messages (dunamis power vs. counting costs) are contrary to one another. Yet I sensed that the Lord was helping me to be set free from a root of bondage that had held me captive for long enough. From folly to faith?

A significant part of the journey to the freedom that a walk by faith has to offer—to truly forgive oneself. What was I still needing to forgive? Money was at the center of much of my folly. Reflecting on an albeit reckless need to interrupt the tentacles of pain stemming from early childhood sexual abuse, using money in ineffective ways (failed attempts to self-medicate) translated into more pain and trauma.

Perhaps like any of you, I did not come from a background of knowledge or understanding about money and stewardship. No one really talked about it, unless mistakes were made—and then it seemed everyone had plenty to say, none of it positive. Most of it was condemning, fueling a result of personal shame on the person who made the mistake(s).

I may be in error about the timeframe, but I believe I was in my early twenties when I first had an idea of having unlimited resources, being able to do much for many. I have learned the hard way that to have an idea is one thing. To truly know what it can mean and how to carry it out, is something quite different.

I am very much aware (at this time of my life) that the idea gave me hope that I could be (in the eyes of others, certainly family and those closest to me) someone that would be welcomed, valued, and yes—loved. Of course, at that age I was not considering that a good many "friends and family" would welcome me for what I might have in my hands. That wouldn't give me the affirmation and unconditional acceptance my heart yearned to receive. No, that would bring about more superficial, conditional relationships that had nothing to do with valuing me—just valuing what I could do or give, a different version of being abused, decidedly not the outcome I was seeking.

Yet, unaware at that time of the negative issues that might come to me resulting from a significant increase in money coupled with a lack of knowledge of how to handle such increase, I made choices that I thought could get me to that goal of unlimited resources. I did not realize how reckless and unreasonable the choices actually were. Instead of supporting a pathway to being able to do all for my family and others that I wanted to do, I was digging a ditch of debt and captivity that brought about more a sense of shame and condemnation, expanded by those from whom I so wanted to be valued and accepted—yes even family and those closest to me.

Let me hasten to add that it is not that I did not (or do not) understand why such consternation would have been steered my way. Why would anyone make a choice to add mountains of debt to their life, and so burden their family?

My answer to that question is this: I don't believe anyone would make a choice to add mountains of debt to their life or financially burden their family IF they truly thought the result were going to end there. The belief, while making those choices (at least for me), was that this is what I had observed as how people did things, got things, had success. It never occurred to me that there could be a way that would allow for payments to be made, wants could be satisfied, and debt would not be the vehicle for having things in life, or as a means to do things for others.

Fast forward. With a nine-year tenure in a local non-profit focused on personal empowerment and transformation for women and their children, I found myself taking a lead moving to and through a process of acquiring a building, taking steps to creating a future that started out with signing my name on loan papers, quickly followed with mounting bills for the usual expenses that will come along with property ownership: insurance, utilities, legal fees, technology needs, facility services and more.

The dream for good that had so burned in my heart in my twenties, seemed to be taking on the same pattern of becoming burdensome rather than positively impactful, and therefore darkened with anxiety and regret. Had I again made choices that would injure those I cared about—rather than give them a direction they could trust, and follow without hesitation?

Then the message... *Count ye all the costs*? (Luke 14:28).

And dunamis power at the same time? How did this relate? Did it relate?

As I sat and listened to the message, Luke 14:28, something was erupting in my spirit, and I knew that I knew, God was pulling up a root that had been lodged in my being for long enough. There IS an expiration date on the trappings of the devil. I knew I was walking right into my Jubilee.

You see, I realized I had never truly forgiven myself for the poor choices I had made in my youth. Here I was again, feeling just as heartbroken that a mission that I have loved, could be compromised by my inexperience, even though I had been seeking to do things the Lord's way for decades. Still, the question had been staunch in my mind—"have I brought this organization, and the people so in need, to a place of hardship rather than hope?"

Then it came to me: one of those messages that is so clear from the depths of your being: No one had come to help me know how to make different choices, how to be a master of money, or be a proper steward of resources, much less Kingdom resources. The cycle seemingly repeating itself as I served in this ministry that had such focus on poverty and limitation, the Lord was extraordinarily diligent to remind me of John 3:16. I am so loved, that my mistakes will never be who I am. Rather, would I be willing to accept His great Love, know that He saw my heart all those years ago, and continues to see my heart now. He KNOWS that I did not make choices to bring harm to others, but to bring blessings and to BE a blessing.

The vision and the ache that I have had for all of this time, is from God. All through the years of folly, He and He alone, had been bringing me to faith. He didn't abandon me when my bank balances were well below zero. He sent amazing ministers of the Gospel to surround me, all teaching the uncompromised word of God, setting forth a prosperity message that I so wanted to believe... and truthfully, chose to follow even if it would turn out to be wrong. I was that desperate to find answers, to honor my word—the word I did give when I signed all of those "death debt documents" that are enslaving and draining. I certainly signed in the shadows of ignorance, accepting influences that may or may not be in line with God's Word. He provided instructions that I followed, not even knowing how they related to scriptural truth many times because I was a baby Christian as I surrendered my life to the Lord. He knew how to embrace the heart of a child, until she could become Childlike.

Dunamis power. Yes. The kind of power that when you choose Jesus as Lord of your life, destroys the old, and makes room for the new. I could not have dug up this root of self-deprecation by myself. I was convinced I had moved on from that choice. In reality, I continued to hold myself accountable, unforgiven, keeping myself trapped.

God says He does not remember our sins if we ask for His forgiveness. He cannot make us forgive ourselves. When we do not, we keep Him from bringing the blessing in our lives that He so wants to provide. Any mom or dad will know how the heart aches to do well for one's children. This heart desire He put into me, is the same heart He has for us—and it doesn't change when our children go sideways, does it? I am choosing to receive my daddy God, an exercise in healing that spans way beyond physical blessings He has in store (we will explore some of the right-sizing I have needed to embrace when it comes to accepting good gifts from one's father).

I haven't arrived. The journey continues. I have just been blessed with this opportunity to share the path I have been following that has brought hope, that has moved mountains, and continues to bring light through the seemingly darkest of days because of the lessons I have learned. While I still so want to be "blessed to be a blessing"… the greatest blessing will be to share a testimony that God's word and His Love are real. We can be dependently dependent on that Love, and His empowerment that removes folly. As we choose to read, study, speak, believe, and honor His Word, we give way to our God moving in—building a foundation of Faith and a future that no longer depends upon what we see, rather on what and in Whom we choose to believe. It's available to everyone, anyone. Let this amazing Grace be released abundantly through the ministry that He has placed upon my heart, wherever my God would direct me to be.

This is my story. I hope it will be a blessing to many, an inspiration that those unctions of positive possibility are for you, and through you, to bless the many in your life. You will, if you do not quit, BELIEVE ONLY, walk into the future that dreams are made of. God dreams are the best... as they are truly above and beyond what we can ask or think.

Dream Big, friends... and LOVE ALWAYS.

Table of Contents

Dedication iii

Forward v

Acknowledgments ix

Introduction xiii

Launching Into Legacy 21

Seven Days, Seven Prayers 25

Power Points! Slides to Sustainability 33

The Future Does Not Equal the Past. 41

The Promises Really Do Belong to Me! 43

If You Aim at Nothing, You Are Sure to Hit It 45

Back to the Beginning 47

Getting Past the Hard 53

Honor Thy Father: *Really?* 57

Nobody Asked You! 61

Do I Stay or Do I Go? 65

When I Needed Strength, I Found Faith 67

Déjà Vu All Over Again 71

Being Imperfect—A Parent's Heartache. 77

Monkey in the Middle? 83

Asking For Help... A Sign of Weakness, or Strength?. . .85

I See You 91

Rounding Robin Hood's Barn, Again 95

Being What We Say We Hate the Most. 99

Can I Really Experience Healthy and Whole?. 101

Friends Through the Folly 105

Recycling the Cycles 109
Game Changer 111
Finally Breaking Through 115
The Christmas Card 119
Instrument Rating 121
Ask Me How I Know 123
Rewriting the End 125

Afterword 127
About the Author 131
Epilogue 133
Scriptural References. 143

Launching Into Legacy

At a point along the path to growing faith, I recall this question coming to mind: *If you could leave any legacy, what would it be, and why?* It tied to another question, *Denise, why do you want more money?*

As I considered those questions, I realized that my answers had been evolving, changing from an idea that more money would make the biggest difference in my life; the wounds of the past would be swallowed up with a capacity to have control in my life, thinking money would be the engine for that control.

Yet many years came and went. The level of income was not moving in the direction I had hoped; was it better, yes. Was it where I wanted it to be? No, absolutely not. Yet, as the years were passing, the yearn for greater sums of money was lessening. The yearn for closeness to the Lord was exponentially increasing. (God has a funny way of being able to catch our attention, and interrupt our own ideas of what's important, doesn't He?) After many years of allowing the message of tithes and offerings fit my own ideas (conveniently never matching anything close to 10%), I began to tithe and give offerings in line with the Word. A benefit was learning about how to be disciplined in my spending, being a better steward of what I did have. Amazing how much more is available with what you already have when you learn about stewardship.

I had come to realize that I was deluding myself to think that money would be the engine for control in my life. Money arriving too soon would only magnify the wounds and separate myself from the One true Healer… Jesus. The reckless choices would have continued. The "holes in my pockets" would have grown bigger and bigger. Too, I would need to learn how to forgive myself for multiplying the problems in my life by my own choices, even if unintentional, and the impact on my family.

The legacy I want to leave? To be a demonstration of what it is to walk with the Lord, to know the fullness of faith and covenant relationship that is ours to receive and enjoy. In this place, to have abundant resources is to be a distribution center for Kingdom blessings, a conduit for Kingdom expansion wherever the Lord would lead. This formula for peace and wholeness for all of humankind, which of course includes one's own family, is the legacy that has need for significant resources. First and foremost, recognition that nothing matters if God is not first in our lives. Whatever time it takes to get out of the folly phases that considers anything else, is worth the effort!

As I set forth to write this book, it was my heart to share hope for those who have been a victim of childhood abuse of any kind, of abandonment and/or conditional love as a life experience, and how any or all of that can and will link to our perception of money and things in this world. It impacts what we think success should look like. It remains my heart that persons who, like me, have had these experiences will know the hope that does exist. They can expedite a healing opportunity for themselves that stems from a simple (but not necessarily easy) action step: to see their future more clearly through the lens of self-forgiveness and the gift of righteousness that has been fully imparted to us through Christ, as Believers. These are not just hopeful ideas; they are gifts freely given so we can actively participate in the creation of each of our tomorrows, with hearts, minds and spirits soaring in the truth that we are forgiven and forever and deeply loved.

Seven Days, Seven Prayers

Have you ever read the end of a book first? This chapter is for you if so! While the background story that shares the ups and downs of the road taken to move from folly to faith offers perspective about how it is possible to move from challenging circumstances to hopeful ones, there are practical tools that can be applied sooner than later that can lessen the time it takes for others to enjoy the experience of turnaround and transformation… No need waiting till the end of the book to learn about them!

In 2020, the year began with a challenge from a Man of God, Brother Harold Herring, who provided his partners with seven prayers, one for each day of the beginning of January—which of course could be carried forward as one might feel led to do. (I continue to pray one or more of these prayers over my life every single day, now in the beginning of 2021. See www.haroldherring.com)

The prayers were fundamental to this journey. I confess that in the early days in the depth of folly, never ever would I have perceived, conceived, or believed that such prayers could do anything that would be truly necessary for any turnaround, much less every turnaround, in my life.

I hasten to share these prayers now for if you are someone who might connect with a place of brokenness, despair, and yes desperation—the very pit that consumed me all those years ago—the good news is, these prayers and ones like them truly are the fast track to healing and wholeness.

The Word of God will *not* return void. It is true that the more we confess them, allowing them to take deep root within us, the more we thirst for time to read, confess, and embrace the Word, for the Word Is God, and God and His almighty Power and Love are as close as putting our hand over our hearts… knowing He is ever Present and available to help turn things around for us.

Will it happen overnight? Probably not. It is my hope that it will not be discouraging when I say that I have been walking this out now for over thirty years. Have I arrived at the fullness of manifestation that I believe the Lord has promised for me and my life? No. Yet my idea of what that fullness would be is very different. I have had a heart for a financial ministry for longer than these three decades. Yes, I started out thinking that more money would make a difference. Let's be real; more money does make a difference. However, the difference I truly wanted was a difference in impact and purpose. Too much influx of money too soon, would have interrupted that heart desire that aligns with being a person of God, demonstrating a likeness to Jesus as His disciple where the works that we do would be truly a reflection of being submitted to Him first and foremost, and not to our own fleshly desires.

Over the years of walking out this journey into faith, I became less and less focused on the manifestation of "things" and more and more engaged and eager for the fullness of relationship with the Lord as the upmost priority. In that place, I could receive things (to include abundance of money)—and things and money would not "have" me.

These seven prayers are a reflection of what has transpired in my life, an inside job by God Himself, to bring healing, transformation, empowerment and great great Hope for what will manifest in and through my life.

All of the lessons learned along the way are now a part of what Joyce Meyer has shared as being a "mess turned ministry." Let me encourage you in knowing that God absolutely redeems time. The fullness of manifestation is unfolding all along; the joy in discovering parts of yourself you thought were lost (or perhaps never knew existed) become the daily indicators that God's Got This… and His plan would not preclude the fullness. Just because something does not happen in the time we think would be best, I certainly learned over and over again, there is a "best" along the way I would have missed if I had had things my way, which would have been a way of "settling" and not actually giving myself permission to receive all that God has.

There is no need to try and make things happen in your own strength. In our weakness HE IS STRONG. (2 Corinthians 12:9) Embrace your weakness. Let God BE your strength. Get to know the joy of being in relationship with the Almighty, which will elevate you to a new place of joy and humility, hope and expectation.

Let your "end" begin with the following prayers—pray over your own life daily. Added to these seven prayers are "prayer slides" that I developed with some amazing prayer warriors who have been an extraordinary blessing in my life. Get to know the authority you do have over your life IN CHRIST.

Would I have accepted this advice at the beginning? *Not at all likely.* Then again, that was the FOLLY part of this story. Consider the end, *Faith*, from the beginning!

DAY 1 PRAYER

Heavenly Father, I praise you that in this new year (2021), I'm headed where Your Word declares I can go, towards success, prosperity, and the good life.

I praise you that as the days of this year unfold, I will be writing a daily story of success and triumph in overcoming obstacle a man or the enemy places in my path.

I thank you that when any problem or temporary setback comes my way, YOU will immediately give me specific solutions in my spirit so that any attempted defeats can be turned into victories.

I rejoice as I commit my actions to you because my plans will succeed according to Proverbs 16:3, AMP.

I praise you in advance that I will have 20/20 vision through the direction and unction of the Holy Spirit, in the mighty name of Jesus. Amen.

DAY 2 PRAYER

Heavenly Father, I thank you that whatever I ask for in prayer and believe that I receive, it will be granted to me according to Mark 11:23-24. I rejoice that you empower me to overcome every attack of the enemy. You infuse me with inner strength allowing me to be self-sufficient in your sufficiency as found in the words of Philippians 4:13, AMP.

Father, Your Word says that if I believe on you, and I do—that I shall do the greater works. I rejoice all things are possible to those who believe, and I believe according to John 14:12.

Lord, I'm giving praise and thanksgiving because nothing is impossible to me and no word from you is impossible of fulfillment, according to the words in Luke 1:37, AMPC.

I call all of this done in the strong name of Jesus, Amen!
Amen!

DAY 3 PRAYER
(ONE OF MY FAVORITES!)

Heavenly Father, in the strong Name of Jesus, I rejoice that
even now

Debt is disappearing.

Lack is leaving.

Poverty is fleeing.

Faith is increasing.

Money is multiplying.

Wealth is accumulating.

Generosity is growing.

I thank you Lord that I have more than enough to meet all
of my needs! I thank you that today I will be receiving unex-
pected checks, gifts, and money.

I thank you for stirring creative ideas within me. I thank
you for opening new avenues of revenue in my life. I thank you
that I walk in the wisdom and favor of my Heavenly Father!

I thank you that this day you will provide divine appoint-
ments and supernatural connections for me. I thank you in
advance, Heavenly Father, for all these things and I give YOU
the glory and honor as I await with anticipation the manifestation of your power, promotion, and protection this day and
every day, in Jesus's Name!

DAY 4 PRAYER

Heavenly Father, this year the enemy's sinister efforts to steal
my harvests, rob me of my dreams and devour my financial

success and destiny are in my rear-view mirror! In the strong name of Jesus, I bind him and every one of his strategies according to Matthew 18:18 which declares my right... my inheritance as a born-again child of God. I command Satan to release my harvests! I'm serving him notice that according to Proverbs 6:31 to release my sevenfold return on all he's ever stolen from me and my family or is even now trying to steal from me. Release my harvest now in the powerful Name and Authority of Jesus. Amen!

DAY 5 PRAYER

Father, in the name of Jesus, I command this Holy Spirit led seed to go where I tell it to go... to do what I tell it to do. I speak that it will NOT return void according to Isaiah 55:10-11 and Galatians 6:7-9.

In the strong Name of Jesus, by the authority of the Word in Matthew 16:19 which says that whatever is found on earth is bound in heaven. I bind any and every hindering spirit that would seek crop failure for the precious seed I'm sowing.

The Word says in John 16:23, AMP, that whatever I ask in Your Name, you will give it to me. Father, just as you planned for the farmer to expect a harvest from seed sown into the ground, I'm claiming my mega harvest over the seed I have sown. I'm standing in expectation for an immediate bumper crop harvest. In the Name of Jesus, I pray. Amen!

DAY 6 PRAYER

Heavenly Father, I'm calling out, exposing, and cursing these twelve sin tactics of the enemy. In the strong name of Jesus, I bind sin, fear, debt, sickness, lack, greed, addictions, anger, hurt, depression, sexual sin, and hopelessness. By the authority of the Word and through the blood of Jesus, I'm binding these Dirty Dozen sins out of my life and the environment in which I live and must operate.

Lord, I rejoice because your desire for me is freedom! From whom the Son sets free is FREE INDEED! I rejoice because you are with me. I rejoice you will never leave me nor forsake me. I rejoice I will not fear anyone or anything! You are at my side. I call this done and done in the mighty name of Jesus. Amen!

DAY 7 PRAYER

Heavenly Father, I thank you that TODAY will be the greatest day of my life. It is a day filled with possibilities beyond my imagination and expectation. It is a day filled with previously unknown opportunities, previously unused potential, revelatory insight, and divine connections. My desire is for You to be glorified in everything I do today and every day in the mighty name of Jesus! Amen.

As Day 7 came and went, the power of these prayers has remained. I have found that when something is supposed to become firmly established, not so subtle reminders come to us, repeating until we finally agree to get on board. For me, at a point now of wanting only to walk in the fullness of faith, the understanding of "covenant" has become a focal point of the walk. The thing is, understanding covenant and all that it means to be set free from all the folly of life before accepting Christ and learning how to walk in His Righteousness, is the priority understanding we need to experience all that God has for each and every one of us.

Having a prayer team that are warriors in faith and their commitment to being all that they are created to be in Christ, has been an essential part of knowing about and living more faith than folly. The 7 Days of Prayer became a step into a comprehensive daily focus on lifting up prayers over specific areas of need, and areas of authority we have, in Christ, and Christ in us. The comprehensive daily focus came together in a very practical way.

Power Points!
Slides to Sustainability

If you were going to create a PowerPoint presentation that could Power Up your life, you might consider including *Powerful Prayers and Promises* that are pointed to the future successes that are waiting for you…

Getting real with God (who sees everything anyway) is to choose to be freed from any barrier or hindrance of the past, and to open the doors to possibility. Whatever has happened "to you" or "through you"—things that were your fault or not your fault, there is a passage to the Promises.

————◇◇◇◇◇◇————

Lord send prosperity now.

Psalms 118:25

Lord, I have not always been a good steward of the finances that I have had. Teach me the fullness of Your way that I might be a Master of Finances, and better Kingdom Steward!

————◇◇◇◇◇◇————

Let my actions be duplicatable by others, that they may have like success!

Proverbs 1:3

It is my heart, Lord, to be a person of integrity and character, a demonstration of Your Holiness, as You and only You can bring true transformation from the inside OUT!

———⧓⧓◇⧓⧓———

Help me to be surrounded by Godly Men and Women, that I may be sensitive to heeding Your Wisdom and Direction. I have ears to hear!

Proverbs 15:22

Lord, forgive me for following my fleshly desires not knowing it was such a direct conflict to aligning with You. Thank You for your forgiveness and empowering through Christ within to rise up to that place of likeness to You, My Father!

———⧓⧓◇⧓⧓———

Our success is designed to bless others, raising standards of GIVING.

Genesis 12:2

Lord, yes, I have yearned for "things" in my life. Now my yearning is for You first, for in You, I can have the desires of my heart, without them having control over me!

———⧓⧓◇⧓⧓———

All grace and blessing abounds towards me.

2 Corinthians 9:8

Lord, thank you for helping me to give up the striving and

From Folly to Faith

learning how to Thrive in You! You said, ALL THINGS would be added unto me (Matthew 6:8) if I would hearken first unto you. Help me to stay focused on this Truth, to become a RECEIVER of all that You have for me, in Jesus's Name!

———◦◦◊◦◦———

And you will be called priests of the LORD, you will
be named ministers of our God. You will feed on the
wealth of nations, and in their riches you will boast.

Isaiah 61:6

Lord, You know how I have tried to do good truly not knowing how to follow You and do things Your Way; as a result I have experienced results of failure and defeat that have been crushing. You have helped me to know, as You have drawn me closer to Yourself that even in the depths of ignorance, You saw me; You knew my heart. The vision and ideals that have been so engaging in my life WERE YOU. I just did not know how to believe and receive. You have made sure that I would learn.

———◦◦◊◦◦———

To the person who pleases him, God gives wisdom,
knowledge, and happiness, but to the sinner he
gives the task of gathering and storing up wealth to
hand it over to the one who pleases God. This too is
meaningless, a chasing after the wind.

Ecclesiastes 2:26

Lord, I have chased after the wind for long periods of time in my life, not knowing that any other way. In the world, it appears "responsible." Thank you for helping me to be freed from the weight of the world, and chase You and in so doing, found out for myself that You do freely provide wisdom, knowledge, and happiness!

If they obey and serve him, they will spend the rest of their days in prosperity and their years in contentment.

Job 36:11

Lord, let's face it. It is no surprise to you that spending my days in prosperity and my years in contentment has been a heart desire. The further truth is though, that I thought that a worldly idea of having things and money, status—would be enough. It has been over these years of getting closer to you that I have come to know that the desire for good things in life is not bad or wrong; simply none of that will ever compare to relationship with You first, and… none of those things would have ever been able to interrupt the gaping holes in my heart, the woundedness of my childhood, nor the tentacles of addiction and sorrow that sprang out of all of that. You healed those deep areas of hurt. You have paved the way that I might have "things and true prosperity," and You said—adding no sorrow with it. Thank you, Lord!

Stay in this land for a while, and I will be with you and will bless you. For to you and your descendants I

From Folly to Faith

*will give all these lands and will confirm the oath I
swore to your father Abraham.*

Genesis 26:3

Lord, you remember when I came back to Pennsylvania from Oregon, thinking I wanted to pick up and be anywhere but back in Pennsylvania. I was being considered for a job that I thought I wanted more than anything, and perhaps more than that, I felt like "somebody." I didn't get the job. I remained in the land, for awhile… I guess over twenty-five years is awhile. It took awhile for me to learn that I am somebody right where I am, somebody to You, and if I would choose to stop needing affirmation or confirmation from people, if I would choose to stop jumping hoops to try and please people so I could get what I thought I needed so desperately, I would receive all I would ever need of acceptance and sense of real value, directly from You.

———∞∞◇∞∞———

*[6] Then the Lord said to Cain, "Why are you angry?
Why is your face downcast? [7] If you do what is right,
will you not be accepted? But if you do not do what is
right, sin is crouching at your door; it desires to have
you, but you must rule over it."*

Genesis 4:6-7

Lord, I have surely learned that what is right, is what is right in Your sight, no matter what may be tolerated or accepted by the world. I have found that Your higher standard is the place where anyone can become the very best of who they would ever want to be. Making the quality decision to settle for nothing less than doing what is right according to Your Word, is a pathway of accepting oneself, valuing and loving oneself—which in turn opens the door to receiving acceptance from others. Thank you, Lord, for the clear instructions You have given to live this life in acceptance and the fullness of love.

Give, and it will be given to you. A good measure, pressed down, shaken together, and running over, will be poured into your lap. For with the measure you use, it will be measured to you."

Luke 6:38

Lord, you know how many times I felt like I had nothing to give. Thing is, I only considered that giving was centered around money, and I had less than zero in my bank accounts. Yet as I would try to drift off into the abyss of self pity, you would meet me right where I was, inspiring me (as you certainly know how to do) to think about how I could help someone else. Help isn't always tied to money. Start where you are.

Thank you, Lord, for helping me to move up and out, and learning that while money is important, Your power to move mountains is far greater. When money started to come, it became a delight to give that too in Kingdom service and obedience. I learned to take tithing and offering steps out of the pit I had created (mostly on my own), into results that included an understanding the principles of Kingdom Prosperity, a far greater result than what the world could ever offer.

From Folly to Faith

No one can serve two masters. Either you will hate the one and love the other, or you will be devoted to the one and despise the other. You cannot serve both God and money.

Matthew 6:24

So, let's be honest. Money was my god. I didn't intend for it to be, but it was. Further the dream that I had on my heart surrounded significant amounts of money. How could I possibly realize that dream if I did not keep money—and "how to get it" in the forefront of my mind. Well, Lord, this was a big piece of the folly of my life that was magnified by the levels of pain and trauma that had been left unhealed. Thank you, Lord, for your word that IS truth—no matter how we might feel, no matter the circumstances. When we learn to let your truth be bigger than the contradictions, things change—and the Only ONE master we want to serve, will be You.

Jesus Christ is the same yesterday and today and forever.

Hebrews 13:8

YES! Something that will remain unchanged, certain, and clear—where no matter what the circumstances, there is a compass pointing north, and we can never really lose our way. Lord, you know how desperately I wanted to live a life that was meaningful, past the pain, productive, purposeful, and yes, prosperous. I did not have a clue how to do that, and the more I looked around me, it appeared I had plenty of company.

Yet, You interrupted all of the confusion, the pain, the hurt, the deep desire to know how to live, and the feelings of humiliation that I had no idea how to do so. I was that person in my thirties who realized I had no inkling how to live life much less a full life, how to make quality decisions, how to be an example that others could truly trust. It seemed like another place of more condemnation and ridicule—when in truth, it was just as you said—Prov 9:10 ... "The fear of the Lord is the beginning of wisdom: and the knowledge of the holy is understanding." A choice to reverence You, Lord, even not knowing how to do that... was a cornerstone of my story, and certainly contributed to the passageway from a life of folly, to a life of faith and fullness.

———◦◦◇◦◦———

I can see how these scriptures (and there are countless many more) tell my story. In the pages that follow, the evidence of how powerful these scriptures have been, and remain in my life, will bring the journey from folly to faith, full circle.

The Future Does Not Equal the Past

We have seen history unlike before
It was as if it were an open door
to what might be, from what has been
Learn we must, to not repeat again.
The pursuit of life and freedom too
Makes clear the path for us to choose.
Inherent in God's children is
A need to express that we are His.
We may start out with blinded eye
Not seeking Him to draw us nigh;
But in spite He kept us close
Gentle in His sweet repose;
Let us climb and sit us near
Our Loving God with reverential fear.
Soaking in His Loving Hands
Hearts thirsting so to understand.
How He transforms with single breath
and plucked us from a certain death.
Into life eternally
Unbound and yes forever Free.

The Promises Really Do Belong to Me!

The journey to faith is one where OUR GOD brings us Home to Himself, and in so doing, we find ourselves—the self we were born to be in Christ—where it is absolutely true: there comes a day when we have need to ask for nothing, for we are complete in Christ. He sacrificed everything that we might be made whole in Him.

I had been mentoring a friend, a precious friend whose name is Aeriel. I see myself so often in her as she seeks to know the Lord, His Goodness, His Grace, His Love, His Healing, His Mercy. I watch, like a replay of a movie of my own life, this gifted woman who struggles to truly know and believe that all that God has promised in His Word are hers. The struggle is so familiar. The wounds of the past are so deep, at times it is hard to breathe much less believe God is with you. And yet in His Grace and Mercy, He plants right before you someone whose faith has grown, who has experienced the Truth that His promises are real, *and they do belong to me!*

From my own story, beginning in the trenches of folly, I was riddled with condemnation, fear, hurt, and a yearning so deep to want to believe the truth of God's word. Yet fear and unbelief would continue to have their way in my life for a good long while. Yes, I would have breakthroughs and think I had "arrived"—until the next bone-crushing reminder would be set before me, pushing me back into the weeds of the past, reliving the hurt, and retreating to a place where my unbelief seemed to be winning the battle of my life.

I share this because as I watch this precious friend take her steps forward, pushed back with arrows of darkness that are sent to try and move her off the truth for her life (as I was), I am blessed to be able to share words of encouragement to her—almost daily—that the Promises are Real; They are for Her, and the battle we must fight is the one to enter into the rest of God's Word, knowing the Victory IS already won. God is meeting her where she is, as He did me—and in spite of the gut wrenching times when sorrow feels like it's the only thing left to feel, there IS JOY in the morning.

As I take you on the journey of my life that is now wrapped in faith and belief in the multiplication factor of God's blessings *(consider the loaves and the fishes)*—MY GOD has shown me where it is possible to receive more food and supply to feed the masses that is without cost or concern. Submitting to His Word and His ways where in spite of famine, the 100-fold return can erupt as do our songs of praise and thanksgiving for the One True God that always delivers on HIS PROMISES!

From Folly to Faith

If You Aim at Nothing, You Are Sure to Hit It

It seems obvious enough to say, "if you aim at nothing, you are sure to hit it." Is it just as obvious to ask, "Why aim at nothing?"

In my life, I had seen evidence of many people aiming at nothing. In truth, I was one of them. Why? Perhaps they did not know there was another choice. Perhaps there is not awareness that there is no aim or direction. Perhaps there was blind assumption that if they just followed the crowd—doing what seemed right to do—they somehow believed they were headed in a right direction and would get the results that were truly desired.

For myself, I had no idea how to aim. I knew how to observe and follow blindly, thinking surely that those older than I had the experience and know-how to bring about best results for one's life.

I had observed generations of family members caught up in the spin cycle of old habits and traditions, enduring the same stagnant results. Seemed it was always someone else's fault, the government was not doing enough, relegated to a "lot in life," or my personal favorite—this is just the real world (better for some than others).

How many times I listened to loved ones talking about hopes and dreams (defined more clearly as "wishin' and a hopin'") like a wish list at Christmastime, putting all confidence in Santa Claus that this year will be the year that the right doors open, and life becomes more joyful and satisfying.

Years came and went, coupled with growing disappointment and an expanded belief that the status quo is all there really is.

The "aiming at nothing" lifestyle became set as the example for others to see, believe and expect. For someone who ached for more, the shroud of despair was not a good fit.

At some point, a recurring message from persons sent into my life (by God I know) repeating the message of how important it is to be intentional about the company you keep and the books that you read (Og Mandino, *The Books You Read*) started to take root. First and foremost, God needs to be in the center of our lives, our primary focus as where He leads, we can TRUST as we follow. As we assess what persons are surrounding us then, if they are not as invested in seeking the Lord and His ways, it may well be time to get a new circle of friends (and maybe even depart from family for a season). This is not an unusual idea, scripturally. Genesis 26:2.

As I reflected on how I had been taught, it was true that adherence to the Word with a support system that taught God's Word and Truth had not been a part of that upbringing. Religious ideas and a sense of "good enough" based in personal feelings and opinions had been the framework that had been carried forward and passed on. This framework opened the door to beliefs and attitudes of limitation and defeat. For someone with a past charged with trauma and shame, condemnation and guilt were multiplied.

As I took steps to learn and follow the Word, I would find that the epidemic of "aiming at nothing" as well as healing for the deepest inner wounds could be addressed at the same time!

From Folly to Faith

Back to the Beginning

FAMILY SECRETS—TO TELL OR NOT TO TELL?

In the pages that follow, I share the journey that resulted in the habits of prayer, Thanksgiving and Expectation to LIVE a Kingdom Lifestyle, a Kingdom narrative—in the fullness of faith. Prayer, Thanksgiving and Expectation (for positive results more than I could imagine) did not just happen. I thought it all folly when I started out. My feelings mixed with life circumstances that could be Webster's definition of chaos did not lend to a natural desire to pray, to being thankful or expecting much of anything good. I had to learn that feelings and circumstances should not be given a place of control in one's life. There's a much better Way; His name is Jesus. How did I get to know the Power and Peace of that Name?

In June 2011, I finally had the courage to address family secrets that had taken up residence in my spirit, soul, and body for long enough. You see, I came from that generation where you did not "air your dirty laundry" or worse, potentially impose shame on another's life who had engaged in wrong behavior, hurt others in so doing, but to talk about it would cause *them* embarrassment. Odd, isn't it, that we painstakingly would avoid shedding light on wrong behaviors that could be embarrassing to someone, and yet in so doing give them no reason to take responsibility for their actions. If darkness isn't exposed, what is the harm? It was a risk to speak up because one of the persons whose behaviors would be addressed, my father.

In a letter to his sister (my aunt), I began my walk out of the family secrets that had so disturbed my life, into the unknown, saying—

Dear Aunt Zee,

This is a letter I have thought about writing so many times. Until my own heart was right for the reason I would do so, it took until now for me to set ink to paper.

About fifteen years ago, desperate for a lot of reasons, I began a faith journey that has been nothing short of amazing—very hard at times—but a journey I would not trade for anything, or anyone. It's the "anyone" that brings me to the point of this letter.

I have told you that I am a survivor of childhood sexual abuse. What I didn't tell you was that there were four people who were involved, one of whom was my father.

I know that in past times, just living with the secret has been the norm. This was the way of handling things that was thought to be right for everyone. Well, it's not for me, and honestly, I don't believe it's really what serves anyone well. Everyone has to make that decision for themselves. I came to this point of choosing to share my story fully and wholly because of my walk with the Lord. You see, the shame and condemnation that goes along with that kind of abuse (or any kind of abuse), brings with it an inherent sense of personal degradation, a sense that you have no real enduring

From Folly to Faith

value as a human being, and that love is colored with an expectation of being treated any old demeaning way as long as some measure of decency is thrown in once in awhile. You accept that that's as good as you will ever deserve, when that has never been the truth—but a distortion, a gross distortion.

I have been desperate to know real love and healing (which I have learned can only come from God). I have learned that while my own experience had extreme measures of abuse, if there was a good that came out of it, I became vigilant about breaking free from that pit. As I have sought God's presence and His direction, I came to see the "smaller foxes" that have derailed others, good people—who had fallen prey to the idea that mediocrity or struggle in whatever area was just normal, when again, it is not.

I have reached out to ministries with which I have been connected for a long time, willing to share my personal testimony about moving from a place of childhood sexual abuse to freedom from shame and condemnation. It has not been an easy journey, but there is hope. Because that kind of open testimony by others who had similar childhood abuse experiences made a significant difference to me in my restoration process. If sharing the hope of healing in my own life can make a difference for someone else, it is what I must do. In fact, it is part of what I feel I am led to do in this walk of faith.

Presently, I have begun to share, still with very few, though that is changing. It was only a short time after my 50th birthday that I was finally able to say the words, sharing with my own mother that my father was among the persons who imposed this kind of choice on me and my life. The other three (involved) were likewise persons one should have been able to trust as a child: two family friends, and a female babysitter.

Just from a perspective that might be readily understood (by many), imagine if one of your daughters endured such an experience at their young ages (or ever). Would it be acceptable to stand by and be silent? In the years when I was four and five, these incidents occurred. It took me decades to be able to move out of the shadows of shame and condemnation and consider the truth: I am valuable. I serve a God who knows how to heal the innermost places of my being, as only He can. Disclosure isn't about more condemnation, shame, and guilt. It's about forgiveness of people while drawing a line of intolerance on choices and behaviors that are not acceptable by any stretch.

To get to a place of genuinely being able to move on, scripturally, we are commanded to operate in total forgiveness, no matter what injury has been done to us. I didn't want to forgive; I wanted the kind of pain and shame, condemnation, and guilt to rest upon the lives of those who did this to me—as I endured for too many years of my life. However, one thing kept me from staying in that place of resentment and vindictive mindset: what if I could actually find a life that was pain-free, that could help me be the person I really wanted to be apart from what had been done to me—and as bad as this was, could be turned around where others might find healing and peace, too?

It was worth trying the forgiveness and faith route commanded by God. As it turns out, I have been impressed with a vision of whole prosperity as I have taken steps of scriptural truth. I know that all blessing is tied and complete when we make the decision to trust God—even when doing so is contrary to what has been tolerated, accepted, or comfortable around us.

Knowing the freedom that lies within the heart of God, there is nothing that is more important or valuable to me than giving away that gift of healing and wholeness and direction that has become my life now. One day, my prayer is that our whole family will know that wholeness and peace—truly seeing themselves as God sees all of us—past the most despicable of choices or judgments we have made, forgiven—and forgiving, as He has given to us, undeserving as we have been at any given time. That is the gift of grace that breaks us free from the condemnation of religion and legalism.

Blessed in His Love,

Getting Past the Hard

As I continued with my walk out of the shadows, I needed to continue to share some hard things with my family, specifically with my three brothers and their families. In some way, I guess I wanted my family to get to know me. Equally, I so wanted to get to know them more as the people they were becoming with real conversations that departed from the stand-by pretending ways we seemed to have accepted. What were their perceptions and realities over the years? How were they holding up? Could we share the possibilities for the future from what we were learning individually from our experiences, and past circumstances that maybe the rest of us didn't know about one another? And so, I wrote to them... again posing questions that welled up in my heart:

> *I apologize for the sensitive nature; none of it is intended to be offensive or hurtful, but rather pro-active to real resolution, the only outcome that makes any sense to me.*
>
> *The best way I know to explain is to pose this question, understanding that each of us now has children of our own:*
>
> *If you found out that your child had been molested or abused in any way, much less sexually, even if it were a relative that did it, would you stand silent?*
>
> *I have tried to accept the idea of standing silent as being right or just. That deafening silence has yielded*

a darker, sadder, more shaming place in my life that I cannot tolerate for my future.

One of the people who has been (to me) an example of someone who has worked through the devastation of that kind of abuse, is Joyce Meyer, a Bible teacher. She also endured sexual abuse as a child.

Somehow, she is able to speak openly about everything as someone who enjoys real healing and wholeness on the other side of such trauma. It is through the talking about the trauma that she has been able to shed the shame, guilt and condemnation helping others (like me) to know that even the direst of experiences can be turned around for good.

I know that motive is everything. It is my hope that you will trust that my motives are not negative. It isn't from a place of wanting to hurt anyone. Each person who imposed that kind of behavior in my life didn't make the choice from a good place of judgment, obviously. Good people fail in their choices, and since we are all virtually good people who have fallen short more than once (not necessarily to the extremes, but short of excellence nonetheless) all of us qualify for needing forgiveness past those moments. Don't we desire belief in the people we have become since and continuing forward. That is my message.

By faith, I have learned that I can love my father, not the choice that was made or the secret that it turned into for so long. Any one of us can get bogged down in poor choices. We can only ever truly move on when we can face those shortcomings and failings, forgive ourselves, be forgiven, and see ourselves as better and more able as we go forward.

I know this would not have been possible in my own strength. It is by the grace and empowerment of God and God-kind of love that I have been able to take steps at all and become a person who wants to be of pure motive and goodness without exception.

I have believed, and still do—that collectively we want to pass along good to and through our families. That can mean abandoning every idea or opinion we thought was right for even a very long time. The well-being of those we love matters more than whatever image of ourselves we thought was so important to hold onto, what pretense we could hide behind rather than getting real with what matters most, for others as well as ourselves.

Each of us being parents now, know better the deep desire of wanting to make sure that we have imparted what is true and sound to our children that they may have the confidence that they can win in every area of life. In reflection, perhaps the "you have food to eat and a roof over your head" philosophy (to which we were all exposed) might have negated some foundational precepts of character, integrity, personal values, being trustworthy and respectful, intentionally working on building relationships—as actually fundamental to healthy, whole, and successful lives.

I have found that learning how to let others know their true worth and value as human beings, freely giving encouragement, support, unconditional acceptance and love—even when it's hardest to do so—is far more impactful. Isn't it those toughest of times that our actions actually demonstrate our personal commitment about what we say we believe? Isn't it when we stand by those beliefs through the tough times that we demonstrate that we can be counted upon to be there for others, no matter what?

As a parent, I wish I had had this understanding and commitment sooner; I imagine most parents do where their family is the utmost priority. Good or bad, perhaps that ongoing growth process, overcoming past failings or weaknesses, is not an uncommon human experience.

My hope is that the process towards real healing and wholeness that has made such a difference in my life might be of benefit to countless others. Simply, that is the motive—to take what has been hard and unfortunate (and that can be any challenge), and let it be turned around to bring hope and help to others. Sexual abuse and the related trauma are simply something that was put in my life; I know the pain, the trauma—but I also know the way back (that has worked for me). I will do what I can to help others know that way back is possible for them, too. The process to healing in fact provides understanding of how to face any and every challenge. Yet, if only one life would be positively touched, it would be worth it.

By Faith the Journey Continues.

Honor Thy Father:
Really?

I am sure there are others who were exposed to family situations that left something to be desired. I am not sure when the words of scripture first popped out as outrageous as I perceived them to be—Honor Thy Father and Mother (Exodus 20:12).

Really, Lord? Do you KNOW what that man did to me? (I am thinking I am not the only person who has tried to challenge God with His impossible expectations!).

Particularly in the years when each night was an opening to the potential of having yet another nightmare that replayed the horrors of a parent imposing his unseemly will upon you, the idea of honoring, forgiving, or even loving such a person was very difficult. Doesn't the Lord, however, have a way of repeating Himself countless many times and ways until you accept that His Word is not going to change, no matter how hard we may think that it is.

To take steps into submitting to His Word, I wrote a letter to my father with a motivation to begin speaking through all the brokenness that had been emerging as I finally had started to be open about the abuse, allowing myself to begin separating from the shame and guilt.

As a parent myself at the time (with children at home), it made sense to me that if a child (at any age) were speaking up about abuse, an invested parent would be eager to speak with the child and work through the matter. There would be an interest to ensure the wellbeing of the child, even an adult child.

The response did not come as I thought. Rather insults and dispersion were cast with invested attempt to muddy my credibility—to include within the family. One person even chimed in asking "are you sure you have not suffered from foggy memory?"

I experienced the nature of how things were handled at a time when "such things" were not discussed openly out of fear that someone's life could be damaged with such exposed information and/or out of the "seeming compassion" that if the skeletons remained in the closet, it was really best for everyone. Everyone? It was popular advice to tell victims to "just let it go" so you can move on with your life. I don't think a victim to abuse would ever consider this "advice" much less offer it as such.

None of this would ever change the truth. The twisted idea of compassion would only compound the sense of shame and guilt someone feels who has been sexually abused. Still, if Honor Thy Father were a command without exception, and God has given the command, I had been learning He does not command that which He does not empower to achieve.

When you go to God with a request for help and do so with an open invitation for Him to also show you YOU so He can truly help you move past given barriers in your life, that invitation may return with what seems like an even deeper cut than the wound you are looking to heal! God showed me my own behavior in the lives of others, to include the lives of my children. The heartbreak was more real than I thought I could bear. Of course, the intention was not to impose hurt on my children while looking to find relief from the pain in my own life.

As has been shared many times in my life, *hurting people hurt people*. When you are inclined to beat yourself up, the pain of knowing you have been hurtful to others (even unintentionally) is fuel for an already toxic fire. How could I forgive myself? Could my children forgive me?

Honor Thy Father. Perhaps it has taken until even this writing for me to capture the essence of what that really means. My eyes were blinded by the behaviors and choices that my father made that were so hurtful in my life, to the point where seeing any good at all was beyond difficult. It felt impossible. But God. I had not passed on the sin of sexual perversion into the lives of my children. How easy it is to look at our own areas of sin and find them "less wrong or hurtful" than those of others, right? It took me a good long while to let God do the necessary work in me to let go of that haughty idea and make room for His healing power to bring restoration to my heart, letting that agape love bring forth a desire to truly forgive, realizing I was no more or less in need of Jesus in my life.

Nobody Asked You!

Let me share that I have not always known when to keep what I know to myself, until such time as I am directed by God Himself to speak up. In cases where the information may be uncomfortable, not to mention potentially unwanted, God's direction and timing for sharing are worth the wait.

Discerning God's direction is critical for when we make choices. When we are seeking to be obedient in our actions, our motives will be pure. If we jump ahead of His direction, we may want to inquire of ourselves: What's in this for me?

When God does direct, it may not always be the easy thing to do. However, rather than giving ourselves a pass to say or do nothing, we might find it useful to ask ourselves:

Would you prefer to have someone who has right and purposeful information that can make a difference in your life risk sharing it with you (though you did not ask for it) or ask for advice and get information that you don't even know is accurate or purposeful, but perhaps have assumed that it would be?

Not everybody who offers up advice and information without our asking is trying to "control" us or interfere in our lives. Neither has information and advice that we did ask for been correct, useful or purposeful 100% of the time.

Are we willing to ask ourselves if we will open our ears to hear truth even if and when it is hard? Are we willing to be open to considering that our own thoughts and ideas while perhaps not wrong, may not be best? Are we willing on any given day to being open to learn and grow rather than maybe choosing to stubbornly stay in a posture of needing to be right?

I realized some time ago that the habits of anger, suspiciousness, finger-pointing, blaming and other like negativity were pervasive around me, even among family. Was that kind of exchange normal or necessary? It cannot be changed without speaking to the fact that the problems have existed, so that adjustments in choices can be made by all who might desire healthier and more whole relationships (certainly as family members). *Letting something go* perhaps isn't about pretending we're bigger than the problems when we "ignore it" but rather facing them head on so that repeat performances are halted. Addressing negatives does not mean that no positives existed. It does mean we can make intentional choices to interrupt the negatives consequently expanding the positives, benefitting everyone.

This isn't about casting blame. There are countless many examples in my experience over the years where choices in how I and others have responded, behaved, believed—have fallen short of best choices, even decency. That doesn't mean better choices cannot be made.

I had experience with someone who used a strap and physical size in demonstrations of anger. If correcting behavior were the goal, could it have been done in a less aggressive way? If correcting behavior and maintaining respectful trusting relationships were a priority, I can attest the injections of violence did not accomplish an outcome of respectful, trusting, healthy relationship.

Perhaps then it became easy to adopt variations of that theme, thinking it a parent's "responsibility" to show a child "who's boss." Reasonable conversation and respectful relating did not often show up in times when there was no question that behavior correction was needed. Was it really responsible not to maintain self-control so protecting relationship and creating a safe environment for family would not be compromised? Questions like these are worth asking—and answering if passing on faith and not the folly, becomes the goal.

An early mentor (through his books), Dr. Normal Vincent Peale captured my attention because the hope, the zeal, the promise he would be talking about and exuding in his life was very attractive—maybe most of all the personal peace about which he spoke. I had witnessed enough anger, negativity, and an environment ripe for hurt and unnecessary suffering for several lifetimes.

I began to consider the truth that if real change is ever going to happen, it does begin with change in oneself. When we stop caring and concerning ourselves with what anyone else is doing or thinking, choosing intentionally for ourselves what is right & just in God's eyes, applying it in our own life, we learn to be true to OURSELVES. Isn't that real control? Even if nobody ever asks me, I have found that it certainly is.

Do I Stay or Do I Go?

For many years I chose not to return to the town where I grew up; I had been abused there. My recollection of my childhood was fraught with pain and sadness. It would not be until my late thirties that I would travel back to that town in upstate New York, allowing myself to realize that it was not the place that hurt me. It was persons that I should have been able to trust.

Even as I did return, realizing that people not the town let me down, things like child abuse (that I had endured in that place) were not talked about openly all those years ago, but hidden. That culture of "secrets" was not something done "to me." I was just another victim of an unquestioned culture and pattern of victimization that is changing.

The resistance to going back to this place became a lifetime message surrounding the question, "Do I stay, or do I go?" Over the years, situations that were difficult created the same resistance—certainly in my marriage where there was a long battle of religious ideology and my personal walk with the Lord, that is all about relationship and faith. The two are diametrically opposed, and a doorway through which evil can wreak real havoc.

There were points when it seemed like walking away would be easier. (Keep in mind, there is no doubt at times it would have seemed easier for my husband to leave versus staying as well!) Among the reasons I did not leave? One thing had become very very clear to me: it hadn't mattered that someone came from a seemingly "whole" background or a broken one. The same tendencies to confusion, being hurtful, and unskilled at how to work in unison towards a healthy, productive, purposeful, and joyful family life wasn't the norm. Permitting bad habits, lazy word choices, and not being consciously aware of our own choices **was**, regardless of background.

If I were to go—would that be what a good wife would do? If I stayed, is that what a good parent would do?

With God and through His Word and Direction, I chose to commit to learn how to break out of all that confusion, determined to share what I learned about all of it, trusting God that He could see us all through the maze of darkness and ultimately bring us to a foundation of light, hope and joy.

All of this said, I started realizing that I didn't know anyone from any kind of family that didn't have some feelings of being "unloved" or "unaccepted"—or someone else being favored more than another. Finding statistics that proved out that leaving had been a popular choice was not difficult. Divorce rates were at an all time high. Turns out fueling discord in families is a particular strategy of the enemy to all of us. But GOD!

When I Needed Strength, I Found Faith

WHEN THE SECRET(S) LOSE THEIR POWER

At a time when I had just returned from a visit with family finally sharing some things that had haunted me and my life for many many years, I realized I simply needed to say out loud that I am a survivor of childhood sexual abuse. The prongs of personal loathing that had gone along with that, and shame (disgusting deep-seeded shame) had been as much a part of my life as breathing. Until then.

I was learning there is a difference between seeking to truly get past issues and the habit of carrying the burden of choices other people have made that are not yours to carry at all, or yours to judge. In the instance of abuse, I didn't ask to be abused; I did not cause others to make that choice. That is their burden to bear. Keeping silent or keeping secrets have a way of blurring the lines of accountability.

I was coming to understand that I did want judgment in my life, the judgment of God, however, not from people.

God's judgment is about compassion, forgiveness, mercy, and opportunities to become more than we've been. The judgment of *people* is all about condemnation and discarding people as valueless and unworthy of acceptance and certainly therefore, unconditional love. The presumption is that any given person is actually in a position to judge another. That is simply never the case. The invitations to judge are plentiful. Having the strength to resist those invitations, especially when depths of pain and woundedness are gripping, can seem impossible. Where is the strength we need to overcome?

Choose to put focus on the Word of God rather than circumstances. Quit replaying the mental tapes of past hurts. These are steps towards getting in control of your own life with the miraculous experience of having wounds healed, and a rising belief that the future could be bright. Faith takes root; growing closer to God and His ways will open the door to the experience that we can revel in our weaknesses, for it is in His strength and ability we find joy, and extraordinary results.

Maintaining any need for acceptance and approval of other people—even parents, family, spouse, whomever—negates our ability to be in control of our own lives. Having the desire for approval from those we love is not unusual; yet if unhealthy habits have infected relationships, we can inadvertently give away self-esteem and self-empowerment, keys to becoming the person you always wanted to be. On any given day, others are permitted to affect how we see ourselves. If the influence is not producing a positive result in our view of ourselves, it's time for a change. As we take that control back where it belongs by the Grace of God, faith increases.

In the ideal, I think it should be that one's parents, spouse, siblings—would unconditionally demonstrate acceptance and approval of family members even when the choices and/or behaviors may fall into question.

It is always easy to see when someone is at a place of understanding this and applying it. When they do, there would never be any judgment thrown out at others. They know the pain of wanting desperately to be somebody valued, somebody unconditionally accepted and approved of and just genuinely loved for who they are, mistakes and all.

Wouldn't we want such opportunity for ourselves, too? Judging improper actions or choices (if they are *truly* improper) is not the same as judging the whole person. Good people make poor choices. Don't we deserve the opportunity to make amends because good people *want to*—and don't need bullying or imposed obligation to become more than we've been, no matter the mistakes we have had in our lives.

Likely, we all prefer forgiveness and support of those around us, rather than judgment, condemnation or both; yet are we willing to unconditionally demonstrate that level of love and acceptance of others at times when it is seemingly least deserved? When, *if not then*, is such demonstration of forgiveness and unconditional love needed most? If we withhold at the times when compassion is needed most, is that a reflection of someone we may be judging or of our own level of immaturity and hypocrisy? I have had to face these hard questions, as the Lord demands no less.

We are all just so loved, so valued, so unconditionally accepted first by God who gave His only Son without Whom none of us could replicate that level of love, Agape Love. In my search to find the strength I needed to move out of the pain of the past, choosing to follow the Word and apply it, I found faith and more, a growing relationship with God.

Déjà Vu All Over Again

There have been times in my life where I have thought—"I just don't want to be here anymore". *Here,* of course had taken up the shape of various situations and circumstances, geographical locations, and self-imposed definitions of what I thought my life would be at a given point and time, versus what it actually was. My reality was framed in a perspective of disappointment, failure, disillusionment about what I thought it took to enjoy life contrasted with a focus on the lack and limitations that I felt were so extreme and imposing at times it seemed I could barely breathe.

These thoughts and feelings would move me to such a place of desperation that I explored many options for relief: new wave religions, horoscopes and astrology, and blindly jumping into business and financial schemes that I so wanted to believe were on the up and up, only to find myself in a bigger and deeper hole of despair. For those into whose lives I had so wanted to give more, providing opportunities for them that would only expand and grow, was not the result I was experiencing. Instead, the burdens seemed to be mounting.

Not knowing how to dig out from all of the chaos in my life, and not knowing how to really engage with God (if that were even really possible), I knew that I had nothing to lose than to start asking questions to God directly—to see if somehow, some way I might be led out of the pits and confusion, some of which were decidedly self-imposed.

It is only all these years later that I can testify that God did meet me where I was and instilled a confidence in me that there IS power in the name of Jesus… and He, as God, is willing for us to lay our unbelief, doubts, fears… before Him, giving Him the opportunity to lead us into His truth and Promises through Grace and His Love. Our part? Believe. The future *can be* different from the past.

From the beginning, I was not reading my Bible (or anyone's Bible for that matter) but going to church and telling myself that I believed there was a God. Honestly, I wasn't sure what that really meant. Somehow, inexplicably, I would get a thought to do something that I had not done before, often in ways that I thought to be odd and questioned the utility of acting on such thoughts. Yet that unction to take action would override my reasoning. One thing I knew—it wasn't going to hurt to do something new and different if it was legal and it would not push me further into the pit.

By way of example, I was financially in such a mess I feared considering how much money I owed and how compromised I had made my own name as far as someone being trusted with money at all. I was ashamed, feeling so condemned, I just wanted to avoid the realities altogether.

Yet once you start following the promptings of God in your life, fear begins to be replaced with productive action— the action starts showing you that there are solutions.

One day, early on in my journey, I was moved to pull all of the information together that showed all that I owed, and to calculate the total. In the middle of doing so, the thought was coming to me that mistakes contributed to this mess; not making the same mistakes would contribute to the solution, and the possibility of even being debt free!

I put all of the papers in the middle of my dining room table, stood up and spoke:

Debt, you will no longer have control over my life. You are numbers that can no longer have power over me. Your day is DONE.

Seem ridiculous? It did to me as well. But something changed. I started to consider that this *could* be my past, and not my future. This action was a significant contributing step to learning how to choose to seek and believe in solutions over problems. Wisdom was available for how to address life rather than responding, making quick decisions, or reacting out of emotions or fear.

I had come to know that I had been more afraid of living than dying because I did not know how to live successfully, with peace, joy, long-suffering, compassion, and certainly not in an environment of unconditional love and acceptance. Miraculously people were showing up in my life who did know… and demonstrated how their thoughts and beliefs were intentional, yielding intentional and corresponding actions, and further—desired positive results.

Déjà vu all over again? It means something so totally different to me now. Déjà vu depicts an experience that is repeated, often perceived from a negative perspective, as if there is no choice but to remain stuck in a cycle. Now, still seen as an experience that is repeated, it is the experience of knowing that I can expect a repeated cycle of success and over-coming. This journey from folly to faith has shown me that to be intentional in seeking God and His wisdom, the door to best results is always open.

As I reflect on the depth of darkness that was gripping my life for so long, when my heart ached for someone to see ME, see my heart, understand and help deal with the pain, hear the screams that were bellowing from within me... when that "hand up" did not come in the natural, there was a leading, a prompting that moved me to take action. I heeded that direction not even knowing or understanding why, just simple and quiet desperation, like a person drowning, gasping for air. I wanted to live LIFE, but a life that made sense.

In my most recent déjà vu experience, it was very much... *I've been here before.* However, in time, God will no longer let us stay camped out in old definitions. He makes everything new. This déjà vu ended up being an awakening to an awareness that He has brought me into an interactive engagement of walking with Him, submitting to the truth that all things are possible in him/her who believes. As we commit to and are consistent with our daily time with studying His word, His ways, and letting Him deliver us from those old wounds, He is drawing us into relationship with Himself while he shows us that He IS capable of bringing us to a place of being fully healed.

The process of renewal happens all along as we do our part, heeding His direction, learning how to really believe that we ARE loved so much by our Heavenly Father, the very thing we were born to experience and share. If you come from a background of brokenness and hurt, we can find ourselves resistant to believing that pure unconditional love is possible, much less meant for us. If we have the capacity to allow the idea that such love *is possible*, hope erupts—a doorway through which we can be guided up and out of the depths of hurt and pain— into experiences that begin to move our focus from the pain, to the possibility of that which is good, the goodness of our God.

My cry for someone to see ME, know my heart, understanding, explain and address the pain and woundedness? I was heard. That small child within that was looking to be saved... was given a Son, the same Son that is available to anyone who asks... as the bridge to a life that is filled with hope, peace, joy and the promises of prosperity being fulfilled.

Being Imperfect—
A Parent's Heartache

Who would have known that every aspect of one's life would become so raw and exposed when the decision is made to say "yes" to God. (Let me hasten to add that saying yes to God may be more about knowing that saying no didn't work. Even while the steps you know you are being asked to take may be uncomfortable, you somehow know it'll be more uncomfortable not to take them. So, *Yes*, it is.)

Early in the journey I realized I needed something legitimate that could address the deep wounds and hurt in my life. What I did not realize was how much those wounds and hurts had infected so many areas of my life already. I so desperately wanted to interrupt any potential for the same kind of pain or hurt in the lives of others. Yet I needed the pain my own life to stop. I did not understand that my motives were infected with a need to stop the bludgeoning in my own life.

This does not translate to being in a good place to make sound decisions—certainly not as an example of competently handling life's responsibilities for one's children.

I learned the hard way that trying to do legitimate things for anyone in illegitimate ways (albeit not necessarily understood as illegitimate at the time), yields a hurt and a pain that is deep and filled with sorrow. This too, by Grace, can turn into healing and hope.

I share here excerpts from a letter to my daughter—from early 2014:

My Dear Daughter,

I am writing with the hope that in sharing the some of what I have been recently learning might be of benefit to you.

In thinking through how things were when you were growing up in our home in Harrisburg, Pennsylvania, there was a time amid all of the parties & displays of "normal"—that underlying challenges were probably felt, if not seen (beyond the obvious).

I, of course, now understand that I hadn't addressed the root issues of my past. To then know how to be healthy in a parent or even spousal relationship was not likely. In truth, I did not know there was a way to achieve a result beyond what I had observed by experience. I had no idea how to demonstrate any measure of what it would or could look like to be the appropriate example that could be trusted to follow for you, your brother or sister. That was always my heart yet off my radar for how to effectively execute.

(Anyone can do the "to do" list; but relationships demand paying conscious attention to our words, being intentional towards supporting another's growth—where real success then can happen, being principled, goal and solution-oriented. I have since learned that that kind of achievement in a marriage relationship, or any relationship, isn't necessarily the norm no matter what a person's background may be.)

All these years later after choosing to read, study and apply principles and applications of what it does take to overcome root issues, some things have become very clear. First and foremost, as scripture states, I had to be renewed in how I thought, what I believed, and then what corresponding actions I would take. (Romans 12:2).

For a long long time, I thought that the pain and challenges I had felt (through my own growing up years, for example) was due to the obvious dysfunction (my parents being split up, the challenge with my father's sexual and physical abuse, etc., etc.). I didn't want to fuel the same outcomes for any of you. There I was—in a second marriage, then with a baby (while you and your brother were ten plus years older). You saw attitudes and behaviors that were at times most unloving and unkind in the midst of the children I was so determined to protect. To say that my heart ached with feelings of failure is an understatement.

I chose to commit to learn how to break out of all of that junk, determined to share what I learned and honestly learning if there was a God that could see us all through the maze of darkness, ultimately bringing us to a foundation of light and hope and joy. (You may recall me saying we were a family in significant transition.) When I say I was learning if there was a God that could do these things, I had no idea what it meant to actually trust God. I just so hoped that the good of what I thought a God could be, would be.

I started realizing that I didn't know anyone from any kind of family that didn't have some feelings of being "unloved" or "unaccepted"—or someone else being favored more than another, blah blah blah blah blah. Seems there has been some great similarities among people to lend themselves to what they don't have, didn't have, felt was missing—than to be grateful for what was good, myself included.

If you are going to lend yourself to the possibility of a Good God, there must be up front agreement to start focusing on gratitude, no matter how you feel, no matter your personal opinions, no matter if you want to or you do not.

It is a choice, a personal choice for each of us, every day.

The moral of the story—broken families didn't cause that outcome any more than ones that stayed together. What was in common was poor habits: not being clear with words, not being accountable to highest levels of personal integrity and character, not starting with where we might need to improve first but rather launching into casting judgment on others, as if we had no work of our own to do.

We did not create a safe environment, allowing one another the chance to fall, make a mistake, even fail. Isn't commitment about the times when we choose to stay when it's hardest, and in that moment, we demonstrate our true character and integrity? Anyone can stay when it's easy.

While your younger sister was home, perhaps through the worst of the fire and ice battles between me and her dad, she personally witnessed the transition of us both to considering new healthier *habits, stemming from new mindsets. We were talking about what we did want in relationship, marriage, family, and life. Seems so obvious now; at that time, it was new to us. We could openly discuss, could purposefully choose to create a life that we did want, learning that there could be another person in our lives who wanted as much for us as we wanted for ourselves (maybe more). As a result, we would freely choose (free will) to want to be together and build that life.*

We had done a lot of things backwards for sure. As we entered into a time when our youngest child would be graduating from college and we appeared to be "empty nesters," ironically we were better prepared to have a family than we had ever been. I've learned that caring for family isn't a function of who's physically in your house. Family isn't limited to people with common last names. It includes everyone with whom we come in contact every single day, so we will never be empty nesters!

I know I have repeated myself many times saying if I had known... I would have shared differently with you from the beginning. I don't say that because I think you have misunderstood. I say it because if you do understand, then are you choosing to consider a new mindset, conscious awareness, overcoming bad (albeit) traditional habits, etc. because you believe it better for you, as well.

If you are, is it because I'm "making" you change, or that change fits the person that you are better than the old? It is a purposeful fit that brings you closer to yourself? This in turn has you valuing yourself more, needing the approval and affirmations of others less. Yet those approvals and affirmations come more easily and without struggle by default.

I made a choice to change for precisely those same reasons. It isn't possible to remain the same when you consciously choose to develop a different mindset. Right actions don't bring about a right mindset. Right mindsets will bring about right actions. Discerning the difference in anyone can only be accomplished from listening to words. When there is confusion in words, it is evidence of a confused mindset. Confusion cannot yield anything except instability.

Apart therefore from taking intentional responsibility for our words, we cannot be trustworthy people, cannot have wholly respectful and trusting relationships—a prize goal for many, and yet seemingly so elusive.

It has taken us time to learn how to put words and action together in a consistent and healthy way. Maybe we can think of it this way: you and WE as a family were ultimately more important than the pain and struggles of the past, and well worth the ongoing effort.

I love you,

Mom

Monkey in the Middle?

Perhaps you remember this phrase, like I do, from your childhood years. One person would be in the middle of two others and try to steal a ball away as it was thrown between the two persons on the outside.

Yet when this childhood game translated into adulthood tug of war, the enjoyment fell away.

I think I have always had a heart yearning for healthy relationships, so when people would be at odds with one another, and come to me to "take sides", it stood to reason somebody was going to lose. Inevitably the cold shoulder, silent treatment and finger-pointing would follow towards the person who had mustered the least numbers of persons in his/her corner. Sadly, I picked up this habit of how to address disagreements in my own life, as it had been the accepted norm.

In time, my heart ached more *for peace* over having to win arguments (if winning meant continuing along in this way). The tug of war episodes made everyone out to be a monkey (no disrespect to the species!). Out of a desire to be recognized or affirmed, a habit had been created to stand firm in your opinion and argument no matter how harsh or unkind you had to be to do so. Such times had little to do with substance of information, and often total disregard for kindness, respect, loving and valuing another person, even someone closest you.

I don't hold fast to the memories of circumstances that have been unloving and decidedly unkind over the years, most assuredly with family members. Rather my sights have become set on the transformative power of the Word and heeding the direction of our heavenly Father who is well able to bring healing to hearts, and erase the memory of experiences that are not of His doing or His Plan for me, you or our experience with family.

The ideal of what family can be in any person's life may seem elusive because of past hurts and experiences. *But God* provides direction for healthier ways of navigating life's challenges while maintaining healthful relationships, and generations forward can pass along a new normal. The joy of seeing this transformation in our children's lives, and our children's children, is certainly hopeful and heartwarming, an interruption to hurtful chaotic experiences in favor of truly enduring peace, and a transformation of heart and mind.

Faith over folly demands focus. God invites us to accept His Son, Jesus, as our Lord and Savior. Accepting the invitation is only the beginning of the transition out of folly. Choosing to study and apply the word, gaining revelation and understanding is ours to do. What good news it is that the invitation and opportunity is available to anyone, any background (trauma or no) with best results possible for anyone willing to be diligent in learning how to unleash the power within that exists in all of us. There are no excuses if better results are truly the goal.

What is it in your life that matters more than continuing to give yourself permission to not take those consistent steps? For me, it was my children, my husband, my family.

Asking For Help...
A Sign of Weakness,
or Strength?

As I reflect on my life, I can attest to the fact that I lived in the shadows of fear and shame for many years. On the surface, it may not have seemed so, but in consideration of my choices, there was a root of fear and shame that needed to be addressed. Perhaps I'm still in the process of having the fullness of those roots removed, but I'm not where I used to be. An area that needed a particular overhaul? Handling money.

Perhaps others, like me, have had a deep need to be viewed as competent, well-able, confident and ably handling their life. Activities that look like one is well-able may actually be choices that are fueling negative results, even unintended. This is the part of my folly story—surrounding money. From childhood, I held onto an idea that having money was a means to be viewed as having more value, more worthiness in being a friend or family member. Without it, more of the realities of who I felt I was (which was not much of anything) would move people away. An innate sense of personal abandonment would expand.

Still, in the midst of the fear and shame was an idea that money and giving could be used to help others know *they were valued*. At the same time, I knew there was a tendency for people to think that nobody helps just to help and be kind; there's *always* the angle.

Asking for help? Certainly not. That would surely be a sign of weakness or that another person might represent actual value in your life, that somebody else's gifts/talents could complement your own for greater success (together). We of course *can't have that*. The most important thing is that we show how we are able to do things *alone*. (Interestingly, that formula doesn't support value for relationship of any kind with anybody for any reason.)

Every question or request for help ISN'T somebody trying to take advantage. Sometimes it's just good people with good hearts wanting to do and be what is right. Sometimes we didn't get all that we needed to bring about all of the best results (from the beginning).

Where money is concerned, had there been consideration that my motive was not to fail in handling finances, this part of my story might have been very different. I never had the chance to accept an offer of help to learn how to do better, correct the mistakes and succeed.

Instead, there was almost a rallying cry to help people protect themselves from me and the more likely scenario that I was just "trying to get into the wallets" of anyone—most assuredly those I "said" I loved the most.

I will quickly add that I understand fully the quick assumptions would have been made by anyone observing the chaotic choices I was making. It is all a testimony to the need to know another's heart, not just arbitrarily jump to the worst conclusions. Taking time to get the "more" of the story is a demonstration of our own compassion and belief in unconditional love—no matter the invitations to the contrary.

Regarding money, I never wanted more money just to have more money or because I'm all about money. I wanted to be someone well-able to give without restriction or limitation into the lives of others for *their* needs. Seeing others thrive matters to me. Money is a tool to accomplish that. (Just getting a job and having a paycheck and the usual ways things have been done doesn't in and of itself attend to handling money with wisdom or discipline, or for that matter—attending to all areas of life towards best results.)

Regarding the potential for more money: It is just like feeding a man fish. If you give him a fish, he'll eat for a day; teach him to fish, he'll eat for a lifetime. No effort apart from investing time into teaching people how to fish (how to be excellent in financial stewardship—or whatever the need) addresses **the root** of the need—the overcoming of ignorance, learning how to handle resources effectively (resources includes but is not limited to money).

My experience may be in common with others. I was reared in an environment where **giving** or **withdrawing the giving** was a norm for teaching how to be responsible not just with money, but in life. I contend that all that teaches is conditional acceptance of the person based upon how one feels, upon per-formance, at any given time. Add a belief that you have to be suspicious of what everybody is trying to take from you.

We have likely all heard that the only person over whom we have real control is ourselves. When money is added to the mix, it becomes very easy to tell just how far we have come in controlling ourselves, and our motives. What is our intention as it pertains to money?

Do we give or offer help (when using money) to build our own resume, to try and influence another's impression of us in a favorable way? Contrarily when we withhold money, does it include any thread of trying to point fingers at another for their lack of judgment or maturity as it pertains to money? Do we want them to see themselves in a negative way for any reason; let them know they are a disappointment to us because of their poor choices with money?

In the sea of negativity and presumption, how could it ever be possible to consider what it might be like to be someone who just loves to GIVE without expectation of return? (2 Corinthians 9:7)

Is it possible to not keep track of what anybody or everybody else does, but rather to stay true to the kind of person you truly want to be—the heart of who you are as a person. Is it possible to give for the sheer joy of giving, loving unconditionally and being invested in the wellness of all people, certainly family?

These wild ideas have been in my heart. I have come to know they are God-inspired. What God inspires… He will help come to pass!

Asking, giving, receiving, accepting—these aren't perverse when the motives are good.

> *All a person's ways seem pure to them, but motives are weighted by the Lord. Commit to the Lord whatever you do, and he will establish your plans.*
>
> Proverbs 16:2-3

Though I clearly did not know how, I have wanted people (certainly my family) to know it is my privilege (not my obligation) that they know they could come to me no matter the question or challenge. No thing (including money) is more important than their knowing their value and unconditional acceptance.

Things did not start out with this foundation; that doesn't mean things had to stay that way. I have believed that members of family likewise are persons with that kind of heart wanting to be ones that people look forward to calling upon, not resenting or avoiding. *(Exodus 18:21—men (and women) who fear God, trustworthy men who hate dishonest gain.)*

I See You

For persons who have come from a background of pain, abuse, trauma of any kind (certainly from a young age) you don't initially realize how blurred your vision is about life. After years of repressed memories about the childhood sexual abuse in my life, it was in a first marriage when the images started flooding back.

The eruption of emotion, coupled with shame, embarrassment and self-condemnation plagued my ability to be able to function in a reasonable and balanced way. I realized some years later that I had put unrealistic expectations on people around me, especially family, to help me get through the pain of these memories and what had been done to me. They were no more prepared to help me than I was able to understand and cope on my own without some guidance. Who *wants* to know how to deal with abuse situations? Who *wants* to have that on their family resume as a response to the toxins that had been left unattended, perhaps for generations?

As I immersed myself into the teachings of Joyce Meyer (noted Bible teacher), attended conferences where she would be speaking and found myself learning how to allow the pain to be rooted up so it could be addressed rather than avoiding it, the past was losing its power over my present. My future was starting to look possible.

I was learning productive steps to live life intentionally, facing past challenges and even those that were a result of my own erratic choices. Yes, I tried to self-medicate with spending money, drinking, and opening myself up to unhealthy relationships and engaged in the company of persons that decidedly did not have my best interests at heart.

I was digging many of my own ditches. The ditches were getting deeper and deeper. I remember vividly feeling like there was a voice screaming from within me—*Don't you see me? Help me out of this place!*

Yet, the results of chaotic choices seen from the surface do not necessarily move people to come towards you, but rather to move away from you, insuring you are moved away from them.

The voice within would scream all the louder: *Don't you see my heart? I want to do right; I want to be a positive in the lives of those I love. I don't know how!*

It wasn't long ago I was recanting this story with persons who have their own journeys into the fullness of faith and this *Do You See Me?* story resonated around the room.

I was sharing the story at this particular juncture because it was just a short time before that the Lord gave me insight about my life that I had never noticed before. I had used money as a means to try and do things for people, with a motive in part to be valued as a person (not the right reason to give into the lives of others, but I made those choices before more of the roots of my pain had been uprooted for real healing and restoration). The need for acceptance was greater (then) than the reckless choice of using debt as a means to keep trying to "get" acceptance, spending money I did not have.

Seeming like I was well on the road to recovery, having been following the Lord's prescription for Kingdom Prosperity, I found myself at the center of a development project where countless many individuals and families could be served in an extraordinary way.

New to the arena of developing properties, initiatives that integrated construction loans and leveraging resources that could include the definition of "good debt", the bills started piling up and the expectations of what this new initiative would mean came crashing on me like the weight I had known all those years ago—putting my family at risk (unintentionally) with the chaotic financial choices.

A weekend in prayer and seeking the Lord for guidance and comfort, He showed me that I was putting this new venture in the same context of the choices of my past—allowing myself to believe I was putting the ministry I had been serving at risk (repeating the unintended sins of the past).

Then the picture changed. He reminded me of each and every step I had been taking to move away from and out of debt and chaotic financial choices. I had been screaming (from the silence within) for help. No person answered. God did.

The message? **I AM. I SEE YOU.**

God put that heart for giving in me all those years ago. I didn't know how to BE submitted to His direction. Yet, He showed me the way despite the chaos, in spite of the pain of the past, in spite of the rejection and finger pointing the world had had to offer.

I had learned (and continue to learn) from my mistakes how to overcome. I was putting what I was learning into action for this new venture that He was choreographing to bring blessing to a hurting world. By the Grace of God, He was taking the pieces of chaos that had made up my life, turning it into clarity that could provide understanding and hope for others.

Rounding Robin Hood's Barn, Again

Perhaps I am still learning about what are truly responsible choices. For the longest time, I had that mindset that if I would just work harder, do more, jump another impossible hoop, then THEN I would finally see the results I had been wanting to see in every area of my life. Yet as I was learning more about the walk of faith, something did not add up. This albeit familiar but exhausting plan did not ever seem to include a result of living a life filled with joy and peace, much less rest—that God's prescription for life was promising.

I have often shared with people that it is my belief that perhaps we have all given ourselves up to reading a common book that was actually never written about things that have never been true, and yet followed the leading of observed habits, generation after generation, yielding the same unwanted results. Time for a new book that *was* written and does give accurate directions for a fully prosperous life. Choose your version, King James, New Living …

We all have an innate empowerment to receive all that we need by walking a walk of faith (see Matthew 6:33): *Seek ye first the kingdom of God and ALL THINGS SHALL BE ADDED.*

That was a scripture that burned deeply in my heart over thirty years ago… and even now still learning the fullness of its meaning, and its power.

We are openly invited to live in the kingdom now, not later, but **now**. We have to do things God's way; we have to believe God, trust God and have faith in God.

It is by faith that it might be by Grace that we are empowered to receive, not to go get, but receive all that we need for the plan and purpose for which we are meant to live for God's kingdom, and His purposes now. (Ephesians 2:8-9).

Maybe similar to my experience, we haven't been socialized to live *for* anything other than ourselves. Mentally the idea of not protecting ourselves (looking after #1 as it were) though twisted and far from God's truth as it gets, has likely been a universal experience of "normal."

I have known (in that place where we all just know that we know) that I have been walking out a process that is the truth, the way into real and abundant life, if I could really believe such an outcome were possible *for me*. But I was missing something.

I came to know that even in all of the years of study and application and heart to get things right, I was still plagued with the notion of having to "work harder" to get the results I knew are out there, available—and somehow "prove" myself in the mix of things. I was plagued by the "human" tendency (and habits) to be drawn into the trauma of other people (their negativity, bad attitudes, etc.), because in NOT giving attention to such displays, the perception has been that we "don't care".

Is it possible to live without those weights? Yes, yes, it is.

To get there? Foundationally, we must learn to get control over our emotions, and oh yes—that troublesome part of ourselves, our tongues! (Proverbs 18:21).

Not an unusual idea, I desired to be someone who would do well for and by others. I had submitted to an interpretation of that desire to mean that I was supposed to be available to do something to help people in a "negative place" "feel better?"

Here's the thing.

Is it possible to make someone else *feel* anything? No. Our emotional responses do not erupt because of someone else's actions. They erupt because of our own choices to give emotions a priority place in our lives, to include our reactions to people and circumstances.

IF it is the truth that seizing control over our own emotions and attitudes is our own responsibility, then how could that ever be possible 24/7 if we allow interruptions by others who do not choose to exercise such discipline for themselves? I am certainly guilty of getting off the plan of learning self-discipline to revisit that "reliable form of exercise"—*jumping hoops*—to "make" someone else feel better. Hmmm.

The result is the trap of holding each other in limbo… going around the same barn over and over and over and over and over and over… you get the idea.

Then one day it occurred to my "lightning-fast brain" as Brother Kenneth Copeland would say—I can make a quality choice to not continue circling the same barns. Huge revelation!

To digress for just a moment, have you ever thought about how nice it would have been to get these things straight *before* one gets married, before children come along, before you are starting to think that the years ahead are fewer than the ones behind, etc.?

BUT GOD! Our God has His way of cleaning everything up and starting over, even amidst the messes we make, and redeeming our time. I was married for the second time when I came to know how much I needed to "break" from everyone's negativity. In "wanting to do well for/by others"—I realize I had been trapped in a cycle of "negativity vs. positivity," not making that quality decision to go with the pure of the power of the positive (as Brother Harold Herring so often says). The result—frustration, and irritation. In an environment that is mixed with fear and doubt, expectation is infected—and frustration is given place.

Frustration is not of God. Right solutions are. Enter, *SEEK YE FIRST*... once again! Matt 6:33.

The answer includes an awakening to what the grace of God really is. It is all inclusive in answers and end results that we desire (more than we can even ask or think) once we quit trying to do and be everything to everybody, yielding to the very best we can be in Christ!

If you are someone like me who has read the words of Scripture and "wanted to believe" yet found yourself retreating to your idea of what a word or passage meant watering down the truth and its power to almost no effect, consider a new choice as I did: JUST BELIEVE.

When our Lord invites us to be trained up in the way we should go, as a guide for parents—if we did not have that instruction or understanding when our children were small, it's not too late to embrace the instruction, live it and allow God to make up the time in us and through us. (Proverbs 22:6)

We *can* leave Robin Hood's barn behind.

Being What We Say
We Hate the Most

It took way too many years in my life to realize that I was not taking responsibility for my own actions. I was very skilled at justifying them because they lined up with what I had seen and experienced for years.

Let me explain. Have you ever been intentionally excluded by persons whom you love, and therefore know the pain of that experience? That they actually believe that they must exclude you and are justified to do so… cuts very deeply, to the point where breathing seems so labor intensive it is hardly worth it.

(Follow up question—have you ever BEEN that person to intentionally exclude people? Me, too.)

These are surely the times in our lives when we question whether the command "to forgive always" came with the understanding of this unkind, unloving behavior and attitudes.

The choice to cut people out of one's life (until *they* change to meet one's own standards for acceptability) is, of course, hypocritical.

Good people wouldn't want to intentionally participate in anything that would cause harm to others or ourselves. And yet, until we start taking real responsibility for our choices, disciplining our own thought life, thinking about whether our beliefs, thoughts, and actions all line up—we will leave ourselves open to continue to participate in the same negative behaviors and outcomes. In a case like this, we lend ourselves to becoming what any given one of us has said we *hate the most*.

Perhaps you, like me, had a tendency to find fault with others. To do so is to choose to be judgmental. It can be easy to convince ourselves that someone else deserved to be treated with condemnation and finger-pointing, though at the same time we would say that being judgmental and condemning are wrong (well, except of course while I'm participating in it for this *just reason*).

The point isn't to point fingers back at people. It is to point at the long history of confusion and wrong examples any one of us has followed (maybe even for generations). It follows that none of us is in a position to judge people. We are all in a position to judge the choices we have been making. We can choose to assess if the outcomes we have been getting are the ones we really want. If not, we can make new choices to respond and act differently, without condemnation or judgment.

Forgive always and receive your forgiveness. (Luke 6:37). It's a free and healing gift from God. Moreover, by His Grace He can unravel the hurts and wounds we have imposed on others, and those others have imposed upon us. It is never too late for an ending celebration of healthy and whole for everyone, moving together out of folly into faith!

Can I Really Experience Healthy and Whole?

Over a decade ago, I had such a clear understanding that our family was being totally changed around, set right side up. I knew it; I didn't know how, but I knew it had to do with God, faith, relationship, and abandonment of old ideas and "religion."

Have you ever ached for something so much even if you thought it might be impossible or improbable to have?

I could imagine what a definition of "normal" looked like for family (though my level of imagination was pale compared to the imagination of God). I came to know I was aching to experience God's definition of normal.

Being a survivor of childhood sexual abuse, it may seem obvious to say that I wouldn't ask for the abuse in my childhood and I certainly do not excuse it. However, the depth of pain that comes out of that kind of experience, I believe, produces one of two results:

1. Absolute self-loathing and depression, guilt, and shame for one's life (because the addictive tendencies that come out may offer a "covering" for awhile, but the impact isn't removed with any "man-made" efforts to try and "forget" or move on), *or*

2. such a sense of determination that one WILL know healing and wholeness and real normalcy, that any tendency to wrong outcomes will be discovered and overcome, gaining wisdom as to how to combat the challenges that will still come, but no longer have the devastating or enduring impact and control in one's life. The pain can become the *jump start* for moving from folly into faith.

That does not mean that one is immune to hurt feelings or that there are not detours back to self-loathing and shame. It does mean that it is possible to learn how to not let one's feelings or emotions be in control. It turns out, that *is* normal.

All those years ago, I didn't know "how" the major changes could happen. I saw all of the pain we were imposing on one another. I wanted the pain to stop. It can stop. Yet when the habits and traditions are so long in being put into place, it cannot be turned around completely without some moments of additional pain unfolding.

I started speaking up—often to the point of annoyance for everyone. This was construed as me being arrogant and controlling. My intention was to share what I was seeing and learning about those behaviors (which we had all adopted, whether we wanted to believe that about ourselves or not). Still, I knew not one of us wanted to be that kind of human being.

Little by little, I learned to just keep studying, applying, and allowing myself to be changed (first), and to let that example of what can be (with God's word and His ways of doing things) be in the lead. The result is a place of peace, strength, hope and unending possibility.

Asking these questions of myself:

- Do I want what is best for my family?
- Does best include the most healthy and whole relationship with each of my family members as possible?
- Will that level of best be possible if I retreat from letting God continue to do a work in me so I can be the person in their lives I truly want to be?
- Do I think that the interest in a best result matters to my God?
- Can I, or God, bring about that truly best result?
- How have things worked so far doing things my way?

Getting back to the BOOK that renews was not a hard choice. (Romans 12:2) My testimony from folly to faith is absolutely a testimony to the Truth, of Bible Truth, and choosing Jesus as Lord of my life.

Friends Through the Folly

Have you ever noticed that when the real challenges come up, that the actual substance of relationships in your life are exposed? For those, like me, who chose to take the road less traveled and launched out into the deep with a faith journey, coupled with demonstrations of total lack of competency as it pertained to finances, it was easy for some to conclude that I had launched out into the *deep*, but not the deepness of faith. Notions of total selfishness, disrespect for others, using people to get what I wanted for myself… you get the idea.

When our youngest daughter graduated from high school, my mom (her grandma, of course) had promised her a trip to Branson, Missouri by way of Memphis, Tennessee. Plans included minor league baseball, Graceland, and going to shows in Branson.

My mother extended an invitation for me to go. How does this tie to the substance of relationships through folly?

I accepted the invitation, making it clear that I could not help with much of the costs. I was assured that that was not a problem; I was just being invited to go because our time together was the priority. That example of compassion was a piece of personal inspiration that helped carry me through patchy parts of this journey.

While away on this trip, I learned more about what substance in relationship really means. The assumptions that were being made were actually not far off from how I was feeling about myself. This in turn made it easy to allow the assumptions to infect my self-esteem.

In part, I had allowed the notion that if someone was asking for help, they would not be as valuable or "able" as persons giving help. Further, if there was a choice to receive help, wouldn't that mean there was an acceptance to being obligated to the person(s) helping?

As twisted as I knew that was in my head, the feelings of self-worth (or lack thereof) were flooding my mind and emotions.

Then like many times before, a series of questions came to mind:

- If we perceive someone who receives or needs help as "less" than someone giving help, are we also saying that we believe that someone who "gives" help is ridiculous for doing so?
- Are we suggesting that giving "help" (with strings attached) is even help at all?

In the walk from folly to faith, and studying God's plan for prosperity, it became clear that giving **is** a key, and *being giving*—without expectation of any return.

I started to realize that in learning about the substance of relationships that were being exposed as I continued through the challenges in my life, I was learning as much about the kind of substance I wanted to demonstrate in my life. How did I want to respond where others were concerned so that when their challenges would show up (as they do), in their evaluation of who was there for them—not judging, not leaving, not condemning—I might be counted among those?

I wanted to be the kind of person I had so wanted others to be in my life; I think there's a golden rule "thing" that speaks to this! I wanted to demonstrate what it is to be someone without ulterior motives. I simply wanted to demonstrate a heart of genuine unconditional caring and compassion, whatever the need. Even if it were money, I could be that someone from whom another could ask for help... without worry of thinking there was attached any condemnation, shame, guilt, or diminishing of their personal worth or value.

In sum, I knew I wanted to BE the change I wanted to see. I could be a friend in someone else's journey, even in their times of folly.

Recycling the Cycles

Did you ever have the thought that you have lived the same story over and over and over again? Wanting to BE the change I wanted to see was not something that was just going to happen. Rather, I would have these "repeating the cycles" episodes. I wondered if there was truly a way to leave old patterns behind, and experience life differently, with hope, as well as new and better outcomes.

In scripture we are told that we need to let our thoughts mirror the thoughts of God (Psalms 49:3, Psalms 51:10). I had spent countless hours studying the Word and spending time tuning into TBN and other Christian networks finding such joy in listening to people sharing their faith and testimonies to the things that God had done in their lives.

I found myself wanting to expect an experience of the truly miraculous in my own life, yet with returns that were often (sadly) disappointing. What was I doing wrong? The cycles of trying to do more, work harder, prove myself more worthy were recycling in my life with that familiar voice in my head suggesting that *the better results just might not ever really happen for me.* (Then these added thoughts... *to keep thinking that things would be different was a pipedream, and maybe I should just get back to being used to accepting a life that was meant to be limited, and yet lift up praise and thanksgiving, trying to convince myself that there wasn't a "more" that really mattered.*)

I lived in a cycle of wanting to embrace hope, believing there could be a life of abundance and true freedom (John

10:10, NIV). I experienced repeated interruptions with experiences that defined limitations and captivity to negative images of the past.

At some point in this recycling the cycles pattern, still tuning into TBN and strong men and women of faith, I had a new revelation of what it meant to let God's thoughts BE my thoughts. It was well explained in one of the Bible studies with Kenneth Copeland. That is, as disciples of Jesus, it is our responsibility to see what Jesus said, put those words in our mouths, speak them out—and make the quality decision that that word *is* final authority.

Simple? Perhaps. The idea of letting those words BE my words, accepting them as LIFE with the power to change things without me doing more, trying harder, proving myself more—began to settle deep in my spirit. The interruption of the work-a-holic mentality and physical responses to circumstances with corresponding thoughts and words that were part of the "same old" results were transforming. The higher thoughts of my God were no longer distant but becoming real. In turn, my expectation that the *good* that God had planned for me and my family… was drawing closer. Those expectations were filled with a foundation of faith in *that which was not yet as if it already was!* (Hebrews 11:1-9).

Game Changer

Humble yourselves therefore under the mighty hand of God, that he may exalt you in due time.

1 Peter 5:6 (KJV)

If there were a way to impart the certainty that God's word is true, and that when we DO humble ourselves to His mighty hand, that HE WILL exalt us in due time, that would be the message I would want to share with every person reading this book.

While there is no way to say that any given person's journey can conclude in their preferred timeframe or that one person's will be longer or shorter than another's, *it is certain* that if we walk and do not faint (Isaiah 40-31), we will soar high like the eagle, and God will renew our strength.

Who would have thought that the timing of such an experience of being exalted would come during a world pandemic, COVID19?

I had been putting notes together for years that ultimately would make up this book. I found I had one of those plans that amused God. That is, I responded to an outreach by TBN for persons interested in sharing their writing with the potential of being published. Sensing I was released by God to organize the notes and submit a manuscript for publishing, I sent in a sample of my writing. It did not take long for an invitation to come to submit a full manuscript. None of this meant, however, that the release of the book would happen until the timing lined up with God's plan, not mine. *Anyone ever get ahead of God in their plans?*

Not ever having written a book before, I returned to some old habits where I tried to "push myself" to finish everything in time to have a book ready for distribution by Christmas 2019. The holidays came and went, and I was still putting the pieces of the book together. Perhaps Valentine's Day 2020? No. In truth, the priority of allowing God to use this book as a means to share Kingdom messages born out of the experiences in my life to bring hope and transformation to others was being diminished through the habit of "works"—that is, the activity of putting something together to publish, ahead of waiting on the release from the Lord.

I started getting a strong sense that the "end of the story" hadn't yet happened, an end that would actually be the beginning of the chapters yet to come in future writings.

Not knowing that news of a pandemic would soon follow, with a nationwide shutdown in March (2020), the timing of finishing the manuscript suddenly was fully mixed in what it would mean to navigate sheltering in place, social distancing, being considered a first responder in the ongoing ministry work addressing emergency shelter, housing and wrap around support service needs for women and children experiencing homelessness and poverty issues.

How does all of this lend to a conclusion for this book? In what was arguably a very different time for all of us in 2020, something that became abundantly clear: God must capture our attention to bring us closer to Himself. We must figure out how to take that time (even if it would take government order to do so) to BE STILL AND KNOW THAT HE IS GOD. (Psalms 46:10).

At a time when the usual busyness of day to day came to a screeching halt, zoom meetings became a more typical way to connect with others (including family), schedules and our "timing" were totally interrupted where we could not make a plan that did not include knowing there may need to be a plan to re-schedule, and re-schedule again—it was during this down and silent time that I received honors and recognition beyond what I could have thought or imagined.

The one award that particularly stood out? *Game Changer Award.* An award that recognizes creativity and innovation in business, this award captured the essence of what has been this journey from folly to faith.

Having served in the non-profit community for over thirty years, mostly within the confines of traditional strategies and protocols, there had been little recognition for work that was in the shadows of countless initiatives riddled with good intentions but limited in the potential for lasting impact.

Family and finances were framed within the context of worldly ideas for generations, and too often with deadly results.

As the pendulum started to swing rightly into the practice of following Kingdom protocols, learning how to Trust God, Say ONLY what HE says, believing HIS Promises, and ultimately believing the LOVE of God that is the greatest power for empowerment and transformation, results were reflecting that change.

It is my heart to share the Game Changer award with every reader. How? I encourage everyone to *READ THE BIBLE AND DO WHAT IT SAYS!* (Repeated thanks to Brother Harold Herring and Sister Bev Herring and their commitment to sharing *Rich Thoughts for Breakfast* and regular reminders of this simple action step that should be non-negotiable if right results are truly the goal.) Not familiar? Tune in to 1-667-770-1524 @ 8:30 eastern time each weekday morning; Access Code 832936#.

The simplicity of submitting to the truth of God's Word, putting the Word in my mouth, accepting God's thoughts as my own, believing it, standing on it, and most of all, believing the *Love*—was confounding to me for a long time. How could it be that we could trade all of our pain, bad choices, difficult circumstances for life that is filled with forgiveness, abundant supply of God's Grace and His "super" on our ability to win at life, no matter how many years had passed or how many were ahead?

In days of greatest folly in my life, I know I was not lending myself to believing in Agape love; I barely believed in the world's idea of love, conditional as it is.

My journey has taken some time, and it is not over by any means. Simply, if I had dared to believe the Truth sooner, reject any invitation to distraction, who knows what I might have experienced sooner than later.

Whatever the time and investment, I would choose ONE day operating in the fullness of His presence and Truth over anything the world could otherwise offer. In the end, what the world offers is only worthwhile because God's in it.

If you do not know the Lord, STOP right now... and invite Him into your heart. In the words of Ms. Gloria Copeland... *Jesus TAKE MY LIFE and do something with it.*

Game Changing? Absolutely! The pathway out of folly and into faith... YES and AMEN!

Finally Breaking Through

There were many times in this journey where I wanted to quit, yes quit. I found it hard to imagine that continuing along in a way of believing the Word of God was actually ever going to be easier than just having a job, getting a paycheck, being responsible with money, living life comfortably, and convincing myself that I was really okay with the limitations that those choices would impose.

God has a way, though, of interrupting those thoughts, instilling greater desires within us that are very difficult to ignore. I chose to keep reading the Word, keep tuning in to Rich Thoughts for Breakfast, heeding the direction of Brother Kenneth Copeland and so many other giants in the world of faith. I wondered how long it was going to take for me to have a testimony that would be meaningful, one that might even encourage others to risk taking their own steps out of worldly folly and believe that their lives too could be more than they could think or imagine.

Truth be told, I spent quite a number of years in a place of entertaining ideas that real breakthrough (you know, the kind that are so miraculous and spectacular it would have to be GOD) were not going to happen for me. I would create "little successes" in my mind, trying to encourage myself that I was experiencing breakthrough, when I was actually experiencing were more lies of the enemy, attacking that place in myself that still existed—that place of seeing myself as a grasshopper among giants.

I just kept taking steps forward one day at a time.

As 2020 progressed, and COVID19 alone has interrupted so much of everyone's normal, I found myself in a place of greater reflection and seeking answers for the disappointments I had been feeling about this journey that I was so sure was going to be extraordinarily life changing, not just for me, but for my family—and countless many others (maybe even you!).

I asked the Author and Finisher of my Faith, Jesus, to help me understand this "faith" in a way that could help me experience the MORE of the Promises of God, if in fact there really was more than that for which I had been settling.

I wanted to really know the difference between the "wishing and hoping" I had been surrendered to and which had been sabotaging my actual belief in the Word, not to mention real HOPE of believing that which is not, as if it already was.

I wanted my prayers to be productive and meaningful, and certain to be in line with the plan and purpose of God for my life.

Ask and you shall receive. Knock and it shall be opened to you. Matthew 7:7. Perhaps I had been afraid to get real about this. A root of fear still had a grip on me. I wanted to experience all that God had for me; I wanted the experience with a purity of heart and motive however. I had this lingering idea that if I wanted abundant supply of every good thing in this world, it would be perceived as selfish (maybe some unattended religious ideology). I struggled with seeing myself as selfish. I was shutting down my own ability to receive.

The Finisher of my faith began to minister to me, helping me to face the untruths that I had ingested, recreating an image of myself that I could embrace, and dare I say, love unconditionally?

As my spirit was filling up with joy, hope, and confidence, with a growing understanding that I was becoming singularly focused, wanting to be fully surrendered to the Lord, available to His direction each and every day, the reaction from relationships in the world started to take a decided negative turn. Accusations started flying. My integrity and character were being challenged. I was being targeted with unsubstantiated rumors. The work that I had loved was becoming something I no longer recognized.

From the world's perspective, the circumstances were dire and unpleasant. In my journey out of folly, the pathway into breakthrough brought forth responses to situations that were totally contrary to what I had known. I was joyful amid circumstances that looked anything but pleasant.

My heart belonged to the Lord. I needed to do things His way or no way. In the middle of a pandemic when people were losing their jobs, were financially unstable and anxiety was mounting everywhere, I resigned from my position. I had no idea what the next steps were going to look like; I only knew they were with God, and in His Love for Me (which I had finally learned to accept and receive), I knew my time for real breakthrough had come.

In a very short period of time, I came in contact with a Human Relations Specialist who shared her story with me about how she became a business owner, enjoying success for over nine years. Likewise, a person of faith, her exit from the "world's ways" were similar to my own. She offered her services as a business development coach and mentor. A man of faith stepped up to help create a website and attend to the IT needs I would have for launching my own consulting business.

Referrals were starting to be received for my services, and the doors had not officially opened yet.

This book? God was finally writing the end of the story... as clearly new exciting chapters were just beginning!

The Christmas Card

As you begin to walk with the Lord, you start appreciating so much His timing. It is actually possible to stop trying to get things to happen when you think you want or need for them to and enjoy the journey knowing that the timing will be absolutely perfect, and maybe with lessons learned we might otherwise miss.

It has been countless many years since I confronted the trauma of my childhood, facing it squarely as I shared it with members of my family, many of whom (certainly my father) would have preferred were left behind muted.

Messages of disapproval and questioning of my truthfulness and clarity of memory of what had been imposed upon me as a young girl had been free flowing for years. While I had chosen to follow the direction of the Lord and continue to send cards to my father over the years for special occasions, no such effort was made in return.

Then, in December 2020, finally experiencing HOPE at levels I could not have imagined, the mail was delivered like every other day. Unlike every other day, though, was a card addressed to our family. The handwriting was familiar. The return address—from my dad.

For me it was a message from God Himself, that He is working on the hearts of all people, helping us to forgive ourselves and know that He (because of Jesus) sees us separated from the sins of the past.

At no time of year could it have been more appropriate to receive the card. In a season of miracles, and a time through a global pandemic the notion of healing on many levels becomes top of mind. Whatever else might happen in what has been a fractured relationship, I could see forward beyond the broken-ness like never before. I realized that gift had been multiplied many times in my life over the years.

Instrument Rating

My husband is a private pilot. He has been considering getting instrument rated. Understanding that kind of training demands that you trust fully in the instruments you are reading, not sight, feelings, other people, assumptions or opinions, it occurred to me that this type of training is precisely the journey we take as we depart from the world's ways and choose faith.

Trusting that the instrument panel is not faulty in any way and when followed will safely lead you to your chosen destination, any one of us truly wanting God's best in our lives will need to make the decision to trust that the Word is not faulty, choose to discipline ourselves not to go sideways when turbulence comes, because it surely will.

For those, like myself, whose early years were infected with trauma and deep wounds, trust does not come easily. To abandon what we can actually see in favor of what we cannot, can seem particularly fool hearty.

However, when the desire to overcome pain becomes greater than the fear of staying the same, getting instrument rated as a person of faith, can be an easy step to take.

Ask Me How I Know

For anyone who has experienced hardship in their life of any kind, the road to recovery can seem overwhelming. *Ask me how I know.*

In his book, *Rich Thinking*, Dr. Robert Gibson speaks to the need for developing the "positive attitude" muscle—regardless of circumstances or magnitude of a trial. He reminds us of the verse in the book of Proverbs, *"As a man thinketh in his heart, so is he…"* When leaning on the Lord has not been the normal response, how we think of ourselves at the heart level may not be all that positive.

Ask me how I know.

I acquired the full Millionaire University training kit that Dr. Gibson created fairly early on in my journey. I was captivated by the idea of being a millionaire, somewhere in my heart believing that was the answer to all that ailed me!

Many years later, needing to clean the layers of dust off the materials otherwise still looking brand new, I am more ably prepared to study and apply the lessons in his marvelous teachings. Yes, I am still captivated by becoming a millionaire, yet not for the same reasons. I no longer expect money to be the healing agent for my life. No. Rather because my life IS healed, money can be the tool it is meant to be to help mobilize a kingdom army so that others may find the same hope and healing I found in this journey from folly to faith.

Dr. Gibson's work was introduced to me by Brother Harold Herring and his ministry, the Debt Free Army. How often I have heard him and his fine wife, Bev, speak to those of us who have tuned into Rich Thoughts for Breakfast daily for some years now—"Don't Quit! Don't Back Up, Give Up, or Otherwise Retreat!" Echoed in Dr. Gibson's teachings, and equally reiterated by so many teachers and evangelists, what is it that makes it possible to never give up, or give in to the exhaustion and sense of defeat that will come—especially when the idea that we could have a more abundant life has captured our hearts and minds?

Is it easy to choose to keep moving? No. Can it be a daily grind to get one's attitude in shape when the preference is to go back to bed, pull the covers up over your head and let that be the exercise for the day? Absolutely.

Is it worth calling upon the Lord in those times—and at all times—when our weaknesses seem so overwhelming that all is lost, and our burn for moving forward reduced to a flicker?

When the revelation comes that we CAN rejoice in our weaknesses because in those weaknesses GOD is strong, belief of what God has provided gets a stronghold that can no longer be denied. It is in the ability to call upon HIS strength that we *can* succeed. Isaiah 40:29.

The joy of the Lord IS our strength (Nehemiah 8:10) when we finally let go of trying to handle things ourselves, giving ourselves permission to receive all that He has had in store for us from the beginning. To get there demands that we exchange our weakness for His strength, create a new habit of walking in the fullness of that strength which brings hope, confidence and results.

Ask me how I know!

From Folly to Faith

Rewriting the End

I don't recall ever having real dreams as a kid. Wishin' and Hopin'—yes, but no real dreams. I did not know what I wanted to be when I grew up. I ached for a big life and yet could not have been specific about what that even meant.

I admittedly experienced jealousy, had a lust for money, things, recognition, and acceptance (unconditional acceptance as I came to understand in reflection as the years passed). It seemed like the more I sought after all of what I had thought "a big life" would include, the further away it got.

No wonder the foundational scripture that the Lord put into my life as He started drawing me closer to Himself was Matthew 6:33: *Seek ye FIRST His Kingdom and His righteousness, and all these things will be given to you as well.*

I have shared the overview of mistakes that I made, the hurts I imposed in the lives of others (and on myself) which yielded times of despair and discouragement that at times felt would never end.

In the direst of circumstances when I did not know what else to do but to call out—JESUS!—I found myself uttering His name repeatedly until some relief would come. Friends, relief ALWAYS came when I took that simple step to call upon the Lord.

The question had come to mind over the years as to how uttering His name could do anything substantial as opposed to some "action" I *must have to take* to bring about a solution to whatever given problem at the time. Reared in the ideology that responsibility as a mature adult equated to taking some action, not standing still, and doing nothing but calling upon the Lord!

Yet, the response that always came upon calling upon the name of the Lord, Jesus, was PEACE within and a knowing that everything was going to be all right.

In the journey from folly to faith, a glorious result is that the end to our personal stories can be rewritten, and not left to wishin' and hopin'.

Have I learned what I want to be when I grow up? Yes. A Believer, operating in the fullness of faith where everything that I ever thought my life could be, **already is.**

In the journey to this place of wholeness, it becomes possible to be the person we always wanted to be (in Christ) where God is able to make all grace and abundant supply abound towards us (no more toiling!). He *does deliver* real hope and the strength to endure the journey that brings forth a satisfying, joy-filled, purpose-filled life. 2 Corinthians 9:8.

Afterword

In the fall of 2015, God, in His sovereign way, brought us across the path of Denise Britton. At that time, we were in our own transition from folly to faith, from fantasy to reality, and from our own personal expectations to God's purpose and plan. We were in the midst of our own critical transition.

We were the leaders in a church plant that took us from Chris's hometown in Missouri to Carol's hometown in Pennsylvania. We had worked for more than ten years in an effort to build a congregation, experiencing some limited success in spite of the revolving door of families that is typical in under-served communities. Our true heart's desire was to somehow break past the invisible barriers and gatekeepers that were preventing us from reaching beyond the four walls of our church setting.

Through a series of God-orchestrated events, we were given the opportunity to become certified life coaches through a ministry accreditation. Upon completing our certifications, we began volunteering our services in the community beginning with an unemployment center. While serving there, we were invited to attend a prayer session in the heart of one of the most challenging communities in the entire region.

In this prayer gathering, we disclosed our heart's desire. We talked about the unique concept of life coaching that we were introducing in the community; a coaching process that helps individuals and families to uncover and discover what mental and emotional stones are embedded in the walls that they have built around themselves for protection. This coaching style is known as CARE Coaching and CARE means Compassionate Accountability with Respect and Empathy.

Having grown up in inner city environments, and believing that we were sent to Pennsylvania, we came with a mandate from Isaiah 61 to rebuild, restore and renew hearts and homes. We had been praying, seeking, and waiting to connect with the right people at the right time. Another key moment had arrived.

We didn't know that we were speaking the language of Denise Britton who was present in that prayer meeting. We didn't know that we were confirming the process of healing she had personally walked through. The rest is history as we united to bring an innovative approach to human and social services in our community.

We often tell our co-workers, colleagues, customers, clients, and coaches that each one of them is Success in Process. We are not talking about positive thinking, mind over matter, higher consciousness, or the raw pursuit of wealth, notoriety, and fame. We're talking about the lifelong manifestation, revealing, or uncovering of God's answers, solutions and message that is coming through your life.

God connected us with Denise to bring forth a proven process into the hearts and homes of our community. We have worked together for many years now, growing together and fighting for one another through one challenge after another.

One of the things we learned in our process and journey together was that there is a difference between the power of excellence versus the excellence of God's power. Many people seek the power (influence) of excellence which is the affluence that we can gain by performance, practice, procedures, and protocols that are executed in impressive ways. In other words, if we perform well, we can give the impression of excellence outwardly. But the true test of excellence is in the times when we are hard pressed, perplexed, persecuted, or struck down.

God's word pushes us to think more in terms of the excellence of God's power (His presence and ability) working in us and through us; so He is able to attain His favorable or desired outcomes.

According to 2 Corinthians 4:7-9, AMP, "But we have this treasure in earthen vessels; that the excellence of the power may be of God and not of us. We are hard-pressed on every side, yet not crushed; we are perplexed, but not in despair; persecuted, but not forsaken; struck down, but not destroyed."

To be hard pressed means to be troubled, compressed, afflicted, or pressed like a piece of fruit, but God's power within us does not allow us to be crushed, that is to be smashed to the point of being unusable.

To be perplexed is to be in straits, to be embarrassed, or to not know readily what to do. God's presence and power within us does not allow us to be in despair, which is to be utterly at loss or destitute of resources.

To be persecuted means to be made to run or flee, to be pursued, harassed, or bullied. God's presence and power keeps us from accepting the lie that we have been forsaken, abandoned, left helpless or merely trying to survive on our own.

To be struck down means to throw something down or strike it with such force that the intention was absolute obliteration. It's the difference between dropping a bowl and watching it crack versus violently throwing it down and causing it to shatter into a million pieces. A cracked bowl could possibly be repaired, but the shattered bowl is irreparable.

God's presence and power (that inward excellence) is so powerful that when we are struck down by circumstances, situations or even by people, instead of shattering, we bounce!

We trust that as you have read this incredible journey from Folly to Faith that you have been inspired, encouraged, and infused with the excellence of God's power. Now you can confidently take your next step toward victory, fulfillment, and purpose because you can embrace the revelation that you are success in process.

About the Author

Born—May 1958 in Rochester, New York. 1980 Graduate of The Ohio State University with a Bachelor of Arts Degree. Thirty-five year career in non-profit and community development. Honored as a Game Changer in the field non-profit/ministry & community development in 2020.

Married to James E. Britton (of Brockway, PA) for thirty years (2021), with three wonderful children: Martin Michael (married to Andrea Moore Lacki); Marty and Andrea have blessed us with two beautiful grandchildren, Casey and Lydia; Ashley Suzanne (married to Jonah Mooney); Ashley and Jonah have blessed us with our youngest grandson, Brandon. Our youngest daughter, Janelle Louise, with her brother and sister, are blazing their own trails of faith in Pennsylvania and Florida respectively.

Co-founder (with husband, Jim) of *Doing Business Together*, a business development consulting practice, established in 2020.

Of all the education and experiences, none have been so valuable as learning that God's investment in us is so great He could not possibly abandon us. (Erwin Lutzer, in *Walk with God*). Getting to a point of absolute belief and reliance on that truth demanded a commitment to let go of preconceived ideas about God and natural reasoning about what it *must mean* that He would do to show Himself faithful as a Father who loves us best and unconditionally.

Epilogue

When I started this book, it did not occur to me that I would be adding an epilogue. An epilogue suggests that there is a sequel to the story that has just been told. I thought the next chapter would be a continuation of the journey, as if there is a place of arrival that allows you to live with a greater measure of understanding and confidence. What more could be coming with all that has unfolded over these last years?

There *is* a greater measure of understanding and confidence. What more comes? That in that greater measure of understanding and confidence, you realize that there is so much more to learn, so much more growth to embrace, and the journey is unending. More extraordinary and exciting, absolutely!

The enthusiasm one gains from the process is for the growth and greater understanding that is still yet to come—and for what God has done to show what GOOD He wants to do for all of us.

Since the final pages were completed, I celebrated my 63rd birthday. It had been almost twenty years since I had received any acknowledgement from my natural father on my birthday or any other time. It was in the form of a card and signed "me." I can only imagine that it would be difficult to see oneself as "dad" in consideration of some choices made. However, I had reached out in advance of my birthday to reiterate the truth: there is not one of us, in reviewing our lives, that would be able to say we represented the kind of person we always wanted to be, 100% of the time.

In God's eyes, sin is sin. It is not for any one of us to judge the severity of a given choice or behavior of another. That's God's dominion. God has given me the grace to forgive, and to receive the healing in my life that only HE can give. By His Grace, I truly do want my father to receive that level of healing, that he too may know that given choices we have made are not the sum and substance of who we are as people in the eyes of GOD, but rather who we "get to be" as a result of what Jesus did for all of us, IF we will humble ourselves to receive it.

I have come to know how crafty the enemy is as taking our life history and using any given piece to create a stronghold in our lives, the depths of which can take a good amount of time to even recognize, much less overcome. In a world that is consumed with tolerance for greed and self-aggrandizement, being fully separated unto God and HIS ways can take some time. Because of my personal mistakes with money early in my life (albeit tied to trauma issues), I was a willing candidate to add personal condemnation on myself (expert at piling on), with little to no help from anyone else. I know the Word; forgiveness is mine when I confess my sin. Yet in a world where mammon has too often taken a lead in what we serve even when our heart intention is to serve the one true God fully, anyone can fall prey to the culture and habits that are tolerated, even when they are wrong.

When mistakes (particularly at the level of my own to my way of thinking) are made, we can see such errors as particularly egregious, and beyond what we have allowed ourselves to believe God could forgive, or at least forgive easily. All these years later, I have come to know that I was still keeping God from BEING GOD in my own life, a GOOD GOD who does not see mistakes with money as more telling of who we are in His eyes. When we choose to place our mistakes in a higher place of power in our lives, we choose to restrict God and His love for us, to fully act on our behalf, releasing us from our mistakes, and positioning us for the Victories He has had planned all along. (Proverbs 8:33-34). I pray others might release themselves from this oppressive power of the enemy with God's help sooner than I did and receive the depths of forgiveness and restoration God is ready to release, *right now!*

Upon receiving the card from my father, "me," I wrote the following poem. I offer it as a dedication to my father at this time framed in the same prayer of hope: that release from the level of condemnation and torment we might have thought right to impose upon ourselves for any unwise choices of our past be replaced with the appropriate level of forgiveness and love from Our Father God who never stopped seeing us through His Good eyes:

THE EMERGENCE OF ME

By Denise Britton, 5/15/21

I received a card
Signed "from me";
And I wonder
Who this me could be.
Not the actual
Person's name;
More that "me"
Seems not the same.
I've seen the tags
Pops, Jerry D;
Neither reflects

The you that I see.
How long it takes us
to set aside
The need to be right
And gripping pride.
No matter the time
When the light bulb shines;
The future is bright
And the past behind.
A minute, an hour
A day or much longer;
Relationships emerge
Forever stronger.
Happy Birthday, me
And many more too.
You are loved, Dad,
Pops, and Great grandpa too.

In the days that followed the writing of the poem, the further healing and Grace that the Lord extended can only be described as extraordinary. He has delivered me from worldly ideas, toiling and struggling in areas of my life I hadn't even realized had strongholds.

He has set me free, placing me on a course that I know IS the fullness of His plan and purpose for my life.

While walking one morning and giving praise and thanksgiving to the Lord, this message came to me:

Cursed is everyone that hangeth on a tree.

Galatians 3:13.

My great grandfather was hanged for the crime of robbery in the late 1800s in Canada. The journey from folly to faith has its folly roots that span generations. Any family (meaning ANY family) can have a root of folly that takes time to overcome, even generations. However, a GOOD GOD is waiting for us to say YES to all He has to offer in forgiveness and hope, even as the criminals who were hanging on trees, on each side of Jesus. In a moment, even they could be with Jesus in paradise, *if they made the choice to believe and receive*. Luke 23:43.

Just as there has been much to share on this journey from folly to faith, could it be a set up for a story that is compelling and hopeful, sharing practical steps for what it means to be positioned to receive all that God has for us?

The telling of this story began with a key message from a ministry that remains near and dear to my heart, *The Debt Free Army*—shared by Brother Harold Herring and his fine wife, Bev. It is fitting that the conclusion would include yet another message that captures the current place in my journey: a message of commitment. It is a particularly timely message in light of a situation that arose not long ago.

That is, my mother was recently hospitalized (as of this writing). In short, many thoughts and emotions came over me, but one that was truly most telling. In my spirit the question rose up: *DO YOU WANT TO LIVE?*

For anyone who has endured serious trauma and levels of dysfunction in their life, the answer to that question is not always as obvious as it may seem. As I pondered the question through the lens of this journey, I knew that my answer was an unequivocal yes—with the understanding that it is only to live in Christ and with Christ in me. I *found* that which my heart ached to receive: a filling up of such love, safety, confidence, healing and truth through which I can live a life of purpose and peace, a life for which I am eager to respond to the scriptural prescriptions for living a healthy, whole, prosperous life because I know how blessed I am to have been brought through the trials and tribulations by the One who loved me first.

Brother Harold's message on commitment summarized the great compelling that has risen up in my life: to demonstrate my love for the Lord—the kind of love that brings forth a confidence and boldness to live life with reckless abandon, not recklessly. I've done both. What does *reckless abandon* look like?

- Seeking God early every day. (This may not be easy or comfortable at first; stay with it until it becomes easy, comfortable and an absolute delight!) Proverbs 8:17
- Lifting up Praise and Thanksgiving each morning, and throughout the day for HE is with you, the ONE who will never leave nor forsake you! Psalms 100:7.
- Receiving His Power in exchange for your weakness and learning to celebrate your weakness because HIS POWER fills you up— becoming your ability to overcome the world, just as He Promised! 2 Chronicles 27:6.
- Having absolute confidence that He CAN DO what He has promised, and those promises are for you! 2 Timothy 1:2.

As I close out this part of what I see now has been an extraordinary journey from *Pain to Promise*, I realize that the

Power to create flashbacks and new memories has been ours all along. And so, I share a synopsis—

FLASHBACK IN THE MAKING

A flashback can come
In the strangest of hours.
And can trigger retreat,
As confidence cowers.
Yet over time when
A memory shows up;
It's a message to strongholds
That enough is enough.
Backgrounds of trauma,
Evil and more;
Demand the same healing
Of wounds we have stored.
We think ourselves heroes
When we take up a cause;
Only one wound that's healed
Has left another one raw.
We label, we point
And haughty we'll stand.
Not realizing we're clueless
To all matters at hand.
Intentions are good, yet
When Wisdom is nil;
We dig in with our pride
Going in for the kill.
Til one moment one day
We consider this thought;

Have we missed something perhaps
And our efforts for naught?
I have been that flag bearer
towards what I thought was the way;
And a Grace giving God
Interrupted to say
Child when did you ask
Of my Wisdom and Love
That are the tools to bring healing
Born from above?
A world in its thinking,
Disunity brings;
It's racism, you'll say
'Bout most everything.
Correctness and safe zones
Changing of names;
Will never change hearts
And yes whom shall we blame?
In what manner of perfection
Do you judge others before
You examine yourself
Just a little bit more.
Pick up your stone
When you think that you can;
It's the knee-jerk approach
Not of God, but of man.
If the goal is to heal
Then consider this please;
Which color or background
Would you leave with dis-ease?
A new flashback is coming

From Folly to Faith

That is marking this day;
The date and time of Release
And JOY here to stay.

Coming to know that unconditional love, that is *WHO GOD IS* (not just that He is), is a major component of this walk of faith. Certainly, when you come from a background of trauma, confusion and a deep-seeded sense of having little personal value, believing that you are loved so very much that there exists a heart desire for you to live your best life, the idea of being treasured by anyone can be resisted by self-inflicted barriers for a good long while. I'm not even sure how much work the enemy has to do to keep you stranded in the same stuck places, though he certainly will send plenty of opportunities to tighten the stronghold. It has been in the particular holy season of Passover and Resurrection Sunday that God was able to interrupt those strongholds, to bring lasting healing and wholeness to my life. For those reading about this journey, embrace the gift of deliverance that Our God gave to all of us through Jesus, and the Cross. Accepting Jesus as Lord and Savior is a first step. Dare to BELIEVE that you can receive the divine exchange through His sacrifice that is the solution to whatever issue(s) you may be facing.

I spent a long long time trying to figure out how to be a better steward of finances, overcoming the mistakes that I made with money. Yes, I was making strides; however, as God kept drawing me closer and closer to Himself, I came to realize that the GOOD and unconditionally loving God that IS my Father, would do exactly what He said: Forgive. Forget. Reset. In the divine transaction at the Cross, I was given the gift of being DEBT FREE at the very instant I received Jesus and BELIEVED in my heart that my life HAD to line up with that Truth. Don't wait. Ask God to show you MORE of Himself and WHO HE IS, so you will fall in love with LOVE HIMSELF, a place where your answers are just waiting for you to receive, by your own growing faith!

So, is this epilogue a suggestion that there will be a sequel? You decide.

Scriptural References

- Prov. 9:13-14
- Prov. 9:10-12
- P5 Matt 7:22, 11:21; Acts 8:13
- P6 Luke 14:28 John 3:16
- P7 Malachai 3:7-12
- P11 Proverbs 16:3; Mark 11:23-24, Phil 4:13 AMP; John 14:12, Luke 1:37
- P12 Proverbs 6:31 AMP, Is 55:10-11, Gal 6:7-9, Matt 16:19, John 16:23
- P13 John 8:36
- P14 Ps 118, Prov 1:3, Prov 15:22 AMPC, Gen 12:2, 2 Cor 9:8 AMPC, Is 61:6
- P15 Ecc 2:26, job 36:11, Gen 26:3
- P16 Gen 4:6-7, Luke 6:38, Matt 6:24, Jeb 13:8
- P19 Mark 6:30-44
- P20 *The Books You Read* (Og Mandino); GEN 26:2
- P22 1 John 1:19
- P25 Exodus 20:12
- P28 *The Power of Positive Thinking* (Dr. Norman Vincent Peale); Prov 12:1
- P33 ref 1 Cor (Love, patience, kindness, longsuffering)
- P34 Rom 12:2
- P39 2 Cor 9:7, Prov 16, Exod 18:21
- P42 Matt 6:7, eph 2:8-9, Prov. 18:21

- P43 Matt 6:7, Prov 22:6
- P44 Luke 6:37
- P46 Rom 12:2
- P49 Ps 51:10, Ps 49:3, John 10:10 NIV, Heb 11:1-9
- P50 1 Peter 5:6 KJV, Is 40:31, Ps 46:10
- P52 Matt 7:7
- P56 *Rich Thinking* (by Dr. Robert Gibson), *Millionaire University*; Is 40:29
- P57 Matt 6:33, 2 Cor 9:8

CPSIA information can be obtained
at www.ICGtesting.com
Printed in the USA
BVHW031500111022
649159BV00013B/980